water carbon time

water carbon time

Exploring Peatlands in a Warming World

Jennifer de Mooy

UNIVERSITY OF MINNESOTA PRESS
MINNEAPOLIS
LONDON

Maps and illustrations by Jeff Mathison

Published by the University of Minnesota Press
111 Third Avenue South, Suite 290
Minneapolis, MN 55401-2520
http://www.upress.umn.edu

ISBN 978-1-5179-2139-2 (pb)

A Cataloging-in-Publication record for this book is available from the Library of Congress.

Printed in the United States of America on acid-free paper

35 34 33 32 31 30 29 28 27 26 10 9 8 7 6 5 4 3 2 1

Contents

Preface

Human imagination is aroused by the possibility of hidden worlds. In children's stories, we follow Alice down a rabbit hole to discover a wonderland and are swept up with Dorothy through the eye of a tornado to the Land of Oz. In science fiction, we can climb through a volcano to the center of the earth or travel at the speed of light to the edges of the universe. Some fantasy worlds turn out to be more incredible as fact than as fiction: Think of Jules Verne spinning out the tale of exploring the ocean depths, followed by Jacques Cousteau taking us there with scuba gear and a camera.

This book is the result of my own pursuit of hidden places, a personal discovery of peatlands in all their variety and understated beauty. Peatlands occur in small pockets and in vast expanses. They can be inscrutable, difficult to find or to recognize in the mosaic of a varied landscape. Much of what defines a peatland is below the surface in the depths of peat, out of sight. These are wetlands that may not appear to be wet, landscapes reminiscent of the Ice Age. Peatlands hold enormous stores of carbon and preserve millennia of human and environmental history. But much of their richness and mystery goes unnoticed.

My earliest encounter with peatlands was in Ireland, as I traveled through the wild northwest of Donegal with my father in 1988. All along the roadsides were swales flecked with tiny puffs of bog cotton, a kind of sedge that thrives in wet places. The flowers of bog cotton are inconspicuous when they appear in spring, but by summer the seed heads form white tufts that seem to float a foot or two above the dense tussocks from which they grow. Bog cotton dances in the wind—and there is always wind in Donegal—catching the light, even from a clouded or late afternoon sky, so that the cottony heads can appear as a host of tiny candles flickering in the dusk. In my father's cottage near the Gweebarra River, we burned dried peat in a small fireplace to warm the sitting room. The crumbly brown briquette of turf that glowed in the grate was also the organic matter that lay beneath the swaths of bog cotton. The smell of a turf fire on a rainy evening created a kind of alchemy, binding together the atmosphere and texture of coastal Ireland.

All my life, I have loved the solitude of wild places. I studied geography and built a career in conservation, dedicated to protecting and restoring natural habitats. And over the years spent trying to preserve bits and pieces of biodiversity, I began to grasp the enormity of global climate change and how it could unravel all that holds those pieces together.

Thirty years after my travels to Ireland I started thinking about peatlands again. I was working on climate change policy for a state government agency and considering options for reducing greenhouse gas emissions. I became fascinated with the growing research on carbon sequestration in natural habitats—how plant communities absorb carbon dioxide and transform it into leaves, roots, and branches, making them powerful storage units for carbon. I learned that peatlands have a kind of superpower in their capacity for locking carbon in the soil. This sparked my curiosity.

I embarked on a quest to seek out peatlands and try to know them, the way one might get to know a foreign country by listening to the language and tasting the food. In my enthusiastic start to this project, I envisioned a world of peatlands to explore, coastal and continental, across every latitude, from the Baltic Sea to Southeast Asia. A global pandemic threw a wrench in that plan, a complication combined with the realization that extensive travel would result in a huge carbon footprint, an impact I could hardly justify while writing about the importance of peatlands in Earth's climate system. As a result, I narrowed my focus closer to home: the Western Hemisphere. This is still a very large canvas, and I have sampled only a small part of its riches.

We live in a time of momentous change in the planet's physical and biological systems—changes driven by human actions, human choices. In this book, peatlands are the heroes of the story. They are powerful, adaptable, and resilient. But they are also vulnerable. Like every part of this beautiful world, they face uncertainty in a rapidly shifting future.

During my research travels, I was often alone in vast expanses of leatherleaf and bog laurel, mossy hummocks and stands of black spruce. But I was not without company. I was encircled by life, quietly humming around me. I could sense the accumulation of time in these remarkable peatlands. I felt the generations of moss and sedge woven together with the people who had passed through before me, the air enriched by the animals and plants whose lives depend on these ecosystems. The peatlands I was seeking when I began my explorations are not, it turns out, so remote. Hidden worlds are all around us, not just imagined but very real.

Some places live so deeply in our hearts and minds that when we wander into completely new terrain, we can be surprised by some part of its character that we recognize. In this way, I felt the Donegal wind when I first looked out across an endless horizon of peatlands of northern Minnesota; I inhaled the smoky fragrance of burnt peat as I scrambled through a shrubby peatland in North Carolina. In every peatland I encountered, I found hidden worlds both strange and familiar. Quiet places, filled with water, carbon, time.

Glossary

A book about peatlands is bound to include language unfamiliar to many readers. This glossary offers a concise reference to terms used in this book.

PEATLAND A collective term for wetland ecosystems that form peat. Peatlands are generally waterlogged, poorly aerated, and acidic. These conditions inhibit decomposition of accumulating organic matter, resulting in the formation of carbon-rich peat. Peatlands may be characterized by mosses, sedges, and low-growing shrubs, or thinly forested with trees, depending on the local climate, hydrology, and topography.

BOG A peatland that receives water only from precipitation—rain, snow, fog. These rain-fed, or *ombrotrophic,* peatlands are exceptionally low in nutrients.

FEN A peatland that receives water from streams, springs, or groundwater as well as from precipitation. These are described as *minerotrophic* peatlands, as the inflow of water enriches the peatland as it imports organic matter and minerals from the surrounding uplands.

GLOSSARY

Examples of regional names for peatlands are mentioned in the book. The following are only a few of the many local names used in different parts of the world.

BOFEDAL A term used for high-elevation wetland ecosystems in the Andes Mountains of South America. Also known as "cushion bogs," bofedales are dominated by low-growing plants forming an almost impenetrable cover of vegetation that holds in moisture and reduces evaporation.

HEATH A peatland characterized by woody shrubs, especially those in the family Ericaceae such as blueberry. The term is widely used for peatlands in Great Britain and Ireland, though the terms "heath" or "heathland" are found in many places, from Iceland to Australia, to describe dense shrublands.

MUSKEG A peatland found in the boreal and Arctic regions of North America. The word is thought to be of Cree origin and is commonly used in Canada and Alaska.

POCOSIN A type of shrub-dominated peatland found in Atlantic and Gulf coastal plains of the southeastern United States.

A few terms describe the layers of peat at varying depths, the ways peatlands are formed, and how they appear in the landscape.

ACROTELM Also called the "active zone," the acrotelm is the upper layer of peat that lies between the soil surface and the water table, below which a lower layer of peat is continually saturated. In this active zone, water and air can flow freely, allowing microorganisms, fungi, and bacteria to break down organic matter.

CATOTELM Sometimes called the "dead zone," the lower layer of peat is saturated with water. This wet zone lacks oxygen and thus limits the process of decomposition.

FLARK A term used in describing patterned peatlands, flarks are shallow depressions that hold water, supporting aquatic plants that thrive in saturated peat. *Strings* are the low ridges of peat that separate flarks, akin to how the parallel ridges of a mountain system divide its valleys. Both flarks and strings lie perpendicular to the direction of flow in a *water track*, which are channels that form over the peatland surface and resemble a flowing stream dotted with islands.

KETTLEHOLE A glacial depression formed by a melting ice block where an impermeable layer, such as clay, holds the water left behind by the melting remnant of ice. Kettlehole ponds or lakes can form kettlehole bogs, or peatlands, through the process of infill (described below).

LAGG A transition zone between a peatland and surrounding upland. Because the lagg receives water from both the peatland and the adjacent upland, it holds a richer blend of nutrients and minerals and thus supports a greater diversity of plants and trees than the nutrient-poor peatland.

PALUDIFICATION An expansion of peatland caused by a rising water table. *Sphagnum* mosses encroach into mineral soils as the accumulation of peat impedes drainage.

TERRESTRIALIZATION Also called "infill" or "lake-fill," the process by which peatlands develop along the margins of ponds or lakes, gradually filling in the water body through accumulating peat.

PART I

geography

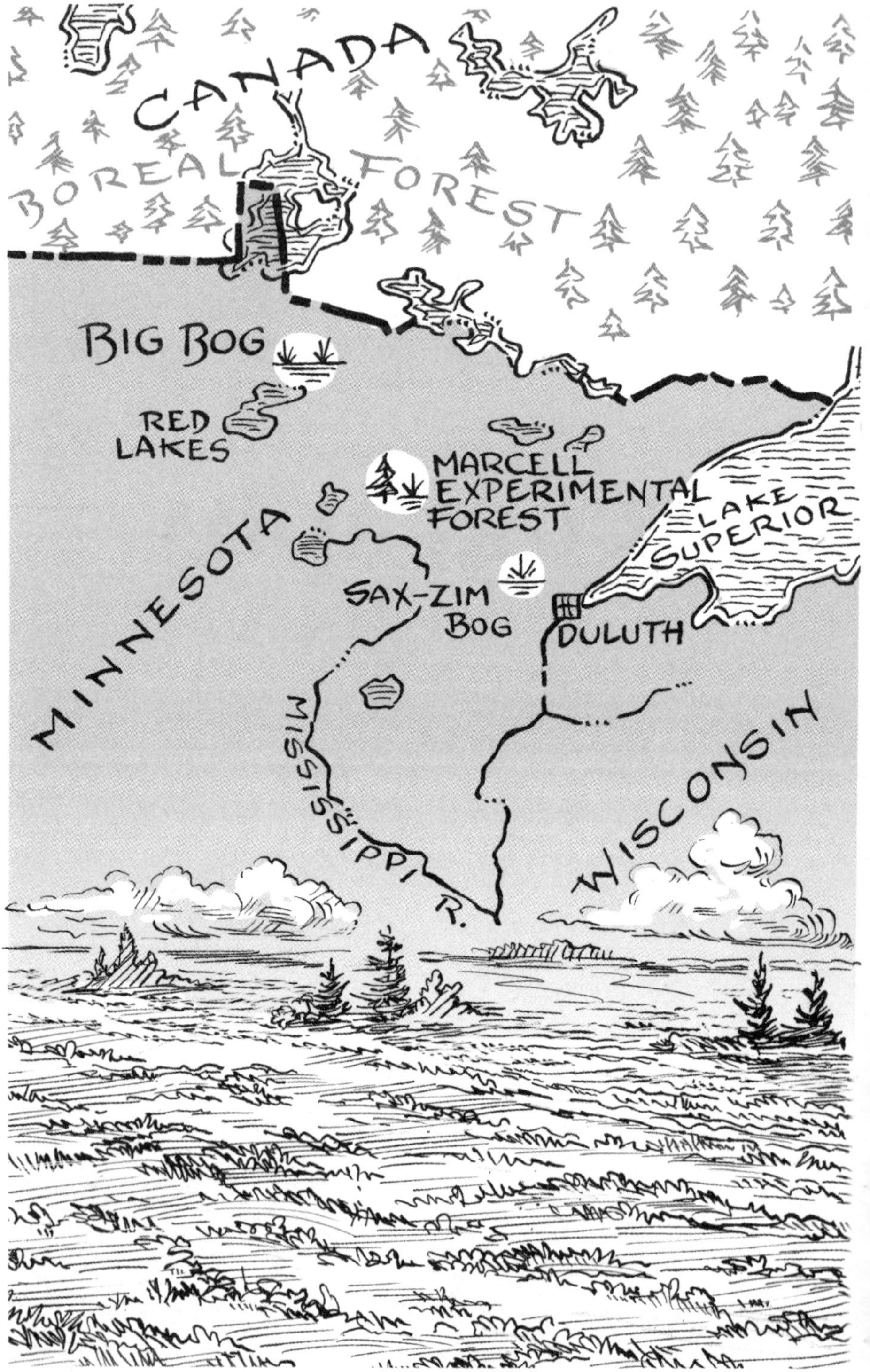
CANADA
BOREAL FOREST
BIG BOG
RED LAKES
MARCELL EXPERIMENTAL FOREST
LAKE SUPERIOR
MINNESOTA
SAX-ZIM BOG
DULUTH
MISSISSIPPI R.
WISCONSIN

ONE

Far and Wide

Big Bog, Minnesota

Most travelers begin with one map and end with another: the first being a wishful image of the places they hope to discover, the second a mirror of the world as they find it. My beginner's map was a broad canvas of peatlands around the globe. At this macro scale, the largest swath of peatlands lies in the northern latitudes: Canada and Russia together hold two-thirds of the world's peat. Yet peatlands are found in every climatic zone on the planet, from tropical to alpine. Bog, fen, mire, moor, muskeg, swamp, and pocosin—the names vary depending on where you are. Concentrations of peat exist in the equatorial regions of Indonesia and the Amazon and Congo river basins; peatlands also occur in coastal and mountain areas of both the Northern and Southern Hemispheres, from Finland to Tasmania. Some stretch for miles, while others lie hidden in small pockets. With this far-reaching distribution as a starting point, I wondered how peatlands are similar or different from one another. For all their geographic diversity, peatlands have one thing in common: the presence of peat. What, then, is peat?

Peat is organic material created under saturated conditions. Waterlogged soils lack oxygen, and without oxygen, the process of decay is greatly reduced. Plants growing in wet habitats produce leaves and stems and seeds, all of which eventually fall to the surface and sink into the soggy, airless depths. Bits and pieces of plants accumulate in this anaerobic environment, building layers of partly decomposed organic matter. The simple formula for the creation of peat is that the production of organic matter (from growing plants) exceeds decomposition—that is, new material is added at a faster rate than old material can be broken down. Anything can be incorporated into the matrix of peat. The wet and often acidic nature of peat helps to preserve the organic material contained within, creating an archive of the past lives of organisms growing in a particular place. This makes peat deposits useful to scientists for reconstructing the ecological history of the peatland and, in turn, for interpreting the climate and environmental setting of the past.

While plants are essential components of peat formation, the physical environment—climate and topography—governs where peatlands can develop. Because water is a key ingredient, landscapes that favor peatlands are those with poor drainage: shallow basins where water collects and outflow is limited, or flat expanses where the water table is close to the surface. Peatlands can form on slopes or mountainsides where precipitation is plentiful throughout the growing season. The abundance of peatlands across the Northern Hemisphere is evidence of the powerful influence of glacial history. The terrain shaped by the melting and movement of ice created ideal conditions—wet, flat, and cold—for peatlands to develop. More than ten thousand years ago, the retreat of vast sheets of ice and the resulting release of water that had been bound up in them was the beginning of a far-reaching reinvention of the landscape.

This transition from the Pleistocene to the Holocene coincided with the migration and evolution of plants, animals, and humans, adapting to a new world as the ice receded. Peatlands provide nesting, foraging, and shelter for a multitude of birds, mammals, reptiles, amphibians, and insects. And for millennia, bogs and fens have supported human communities with food, material culture, and refuge.

Peatlands offer another invaluable service to the living world: their extraordinary capacity to absorb and store carbon. All plants take in carbon dioxide from the atmosphere and transform it into leaves, roots, and branches through the magic of photosynthesis. But some landscapes are more proficient at sequestering carbon than others. Peatlands are the largest natural terrestrial carbon store on Earth. Though found in almost every part of the world, peatlands cover only 3 percent of the earth's land surface, yet they hold more carbon than all the world's forests combined. Small but mighty, these hidden ecosystems play an outsized role in the climate of our planet.

From the start of my journey, I knew of three things that make peatlands what they are: water, carbon, and time. Each peatland I explored was shaped by the dynamic flow of these elements, yet each place had its own character and history. This book is a portrait collection of peatlands, framed by the three essential ingredients. These themes weave together throughout the book, illuminating the ecological and geographic diversity of peatlands; the significance of peatlands as carbon sinks; and the impacts of human action, both destructive and restorative. To all readers of natural history and climate science, these stories offer insight to what makes peatlands valuable—as wetlands, carbon stores, and environments both vulnerable and resilient.

As I embarked on my exploration of peatlands, I was daunted by the global scope, so I folded the peatland map in half. I looked to the Americas—north, central, and south—and found an ecological cornucopia of peatlands. In the Western Hemisphere, peatland known as muskeg is widespread across the boreal forest biome that covers much of Canada. Bogs and fens are common throughout the Great Lakes region, the Maritime provinces, and New England. Shrub bogs called pocosins are scattered along the coastal Atlantic plain, and sawgrass marshes of Florida hold extensive peat deposits. Mountain fens form in small pockets, kept moist by cold temperatures and slowly melting snowpack. Central and South America support peatlands in forested swamps and maritime bogs, tropical lowlands of the Caribbean, and on the windy steppes of Patagonia.

In writing this book, my travels involved a certain amount of serendipity through which I found peatlands in places I would not have expected. A birding trip to the Peruvian Andes opened the way to discovering high-elevation cushion bogs. An afternoon hike on the edge of the Atlantic Ocean led me through a Tolkienesque landscape of pines and *Sphagnum* mosses. I was thrilled and daunted by the diversity and range of peatlands—they seemed to be everywhere and yet not easy to find. I followed boardwalks where I could find them, not wanting to trample the delicate nature of what I sought to understand. But where it was possible to do so, I trod softly into forested bogs, knelt in their deep moss beds, and drank in their fragrant air. And then I sat down to write, filling in the map with their stories.

On a late September morning I stood alone in the middle of Big Bog, like a castaway on an island. The surrounding sea was not one of open water, but waves of fine-leaved sedges that bent and quivered in the wind. Black spruces and tamaracks were scattered across the open bog, short and spindly. Taller trees huddled close together on small hummocks. Clusters of leatherleaf shrubs grew close to the ground with bog birch and bog rosemary. Above me, a high wash of clouds spread to the north, clear blue to the south, scudding cumulus to the west.

Big Bog stretches seventy miles east to west, thirty miles north to south—farther than my gaze could fathom—but still a relatively small part of the larger span of Red Lake peatlands. The continental interior creates a space for peatlands that extend to the horizon. I imagined that, seen from a bird's-eye view, these interior peatlands might look like a rough green animal skin laid out flat: heathered fur pockmarked here and there with smooth patches of open water like bare skin, thick in other places with a shaggy mane of black spruce and tamarack trees. Closer to the earth, the texture of shrubs, sedges, and moss lawns seem to be stirred by a current of wind or water. A flow of green traced a sinuous ribbon across the seemingly flat surface like a hidden river. The flatness is an illusion: Gentle slopes are flanked by low swales barely discernible from the vantage of human height. Water moves slowly through peatlands above and below the surface. Even small changes in topography affect surface water flow, and soil types—sandy or dense peat—alter the movement of groundwater.

Set in the footprint of Glacial Lake Agassiz, Big Bog is part of the Red Lake peatlands of northern Minnesota, a mosaic of raised bogs, fens, and water tracks. This wetland complex encompasses more than five hundred square miles across portions of what is now the northern Great Plains. Some ten thousand years ago, after the Wisconsin glaciation in North America ended, immense lakes formed out of meltwater left by the retreating ice. Eventually, the lakes drained to the north, leaving behind poor dense soils and low beach ridges of sand and gravel. These remnants form the topography that created the patterned peatlands of northern Minnesota that are visible today. The climate cooled and became wetter about five thousand years ago, creating the conditions for *Sphagnum* moss to grow and spread and, in time, forming the origins of the Red Lake peatlands.

Scanning the wide horizon, I could see a subtle shift of colors in the landscape, like a mossy camouflage that mirrors what lies below the surface. Gravels and sands left behind by the retreating ice of glaciers past work to channel, slow, or block the flow of water above- and belowground. Where water travels, it carries minerals and nutrients, enriching the ground for plant life. Where water lies still, responding to the seasons by rising and falling close to the surface, it is oxygen-poor and acidic. The presence or absence of groundwater flow underlies the tapestry of peatlands.

Patterns develop in this setting that are visible from above; satellite images and aerial photos capture the beauty of the landscape in abstract swirls and splashes of green, blue, brown. Scientists have a special vocabulary for what are logically called *patterned peatlands. Flarks* are shallow depressions that hold water, supporting aquatic plants that thrive in saturated peat. *Strings* are the low ridges of peat that separate flarks, reminiscent of how the parallel ridges of a mountain system divide its valleys. Both flarks and strings lie perpendicular to the direction of flow in a *water track*—channels that form over the peatland surface, resembling a flowing stream dotted with islands. Seen from above, flarks and strings spread out in narrow bands that radiate downslope. Forested ridges develop on strings where the hummocky peat can support black spruce.

The platform on which I floated in the midst of Big Bog was the terminus of a mile-long boardwalk. The elevated metal-grate walkway is designed for durability, protecting the wetland vegetation while allowing access into the bog interior. Along the way, I passed through subtle shifts in the mood and character of the peatland. In places, the boardwalk was flanked by dense shrubs and trees that rose fifteen feet or more above me. I passed over a wooded island where black spruces have managed to claim enough ground to sustain a small patch of forest. The trees displayed an odd growth pattern: The branches sprouted densely from the trunk, then thinned out toward the crown where, at the very top, a cluster of needles formed a lush green plume like a decorative topknot. Farther on, the spruce and tamarack trees shrank to waist height and the view opened up like a wide-angle lens. Wiry sedge leaves sprang up through a carpet of mosses, interlaced with trailing strands of diminutive cranberry.

At a midpoint in the boardwalk, I stopped at a juncture of sorts. In either direction, a distinctly linear swath of sedges ran perpendicular to the path like a railroad crossing. It was not the scar of a roadway but the lingering trace of a drainage ditch, dug into the peatlands more than a century before. In the early 1900s, the Red Lake peatlands were the focus of an extensive drainage program, launched in hopes of creating farmland for homesteaders. Between 1905 and 1922, fifteen hundred miles of ditches were created, neatly laid out along a grid of square-mile sections. The state had hoped that the federal government would pay for the project, but the estimated two million dollars was too much for Congress. Instead, the cost of the drainage program was borne by the northern Minnesota counties hoping to see agriculture bring economic growth. The plan failed miserably: Farmers found the soils still too wet to grow crops and abandoned their hardscrabble efforts. By the early 1930s, the counties teetered on bankruptcy from ditch debts, compounded by the national crisis of the Great Depression. The state of Minnesota bailed out the counties in 1932 and took ownership of the debt-ridden lands.

The massive ditch project was not the only attempt to drain, develop, and divide the Red Lake peatlands. Peat has been mined for use as a horticulture product; forested peatlands have been drained and logged. Various schemes to excavate or alter the landscape were proposed or attempted throughout the twentieth century, fueled by the notion that peatlands represented either a wasteland to be reclaimed or a vast treasure of natural resources to be exploited. Ideas were conceived for a variety of economic uses. During the energy crisis of the 1970s, interest in alternative energy sources spurred research into gasification methods that could utilize peat, an abundant but overlooked resource. In 1975 the Minnesota Gas Company requested a lease of three hundred thousand acres of state-owned peatland for the purpose of mining peat as a fuel source. The application prompted the creation of the state's Peat Program within its Department of Natural Resources to study the economic and environmental impacts of the development proposals. Through the 1980s, the state legislature continued to fund projects to test the feasibility of peat energy. While many of the technological challenges could be addressed, plans for large-scale energy development simply didn't compete with current prices and availability of coal.

The Minnesota Peat Program undertook a survey of the state's peatlands, starting in the 1970s, and supported considerable research into the poorly understood ecology and hydrology of the unique patterned peatland ecosystem. The results of the Peat Program studies are collected in one classic volume, *The Patterned Peatlands of Minnesota,* published by the University of Minnesota Press in 1992. One of the impressive features of the book is a set of color plates that includes Landsat images, infrared aerial photos, and color photos taken above the Red Lake peatlands. The images are striking, with the shape of water and its influence above- and belowground illustrated in swirls and waves across the landscape. In the infrared photos, water tracks appear as a dark green current, dotted with teardrop-shaped islands of tamarack trees. Ovals of brown and tan outline the raised bogs flanked by lawns of moss and sedge. Bog islands with horseshoe rings of forest are captured in tones of turquoise and plum. Without the false color of infrared, the images still convey the remarkable beauty of patterned peatlands in their strings and flarks and tree islands. What is also visible in these aerial views is the tattoo of grid lines left on the landscape, the imprint of ditching and draining still healing after a hundred years.

Efforts to divide and conquer the landscape have involved legal and political tools as well as machines, with a long and dark history in the repeated attempts to remove the people who rightfully claim the Red Lakes area as their native home. Two thousand years ago, early Indigenous people of the Blackduck culture settled in villages near Big Bog and lived there for more than a millennium; Dakota tribes also arrived during that period to mix with or supplant the first inhabitants. In the 1700s, Ojibwe people moved west into present-day Minnesota and established villages around Upper and Lower Red Lakes. As Europeans spread across the Great Lakes region, the pursuit of furs and timber and the growing desire for land began to encroach into northern Minnesota despite its relative isolation. The Red Lake Reservation was established by treaty in 1863, but under the 1889 Nelson Act, the Red Lake Band (formally recognized as the Red Lake Band of Chippewa Indians) was forced to cede a large acreage to the north and west to safeguard their lands around Upper and Lower Red Lakes—lands that had never left tribal control. Remarkably, Indigenous leaders resisted pressure to divide reservation lands into individual allotments, maintaining communal rather than private ownership. The Red Lake Reservation continues to hold the unique status of the only "closed reservation" in Minnesota: contiguous, unallotted tribal lands held in common for all tribal members.

Communal governance and stewardship are a fundamental part of the history of the Red Lake people. For more than fifty years, Red Lake leaders have opposed drainage projects, proposals to mine peat for energy production, and plans to alter water levels in Red Lake, all actions that would threaten spawning grounds for fish and degrade water quality. The Red Lake Band not only defends against negative impacts, they also plan for long-term sustainability, producing a Climate Adaptation Plan in 2014 and a Wetland Program Plan in 2024, among others. Their management of the fishery in Lower Red Lake has restored walleye populations from near-collapse in the 1990s to recovery. The abundance of nature—forests and fisheries, cranberries and wild rice, beaver and muskrat—has sustained them for generations. And, hopefully, for many generations to come.

From the evolution of glacial barrens to the patterned peatlands that exist today, forces of nature and people have exerted their influence on the landscape. The one essential thread that runs through the story of Big Bog is water—its ebb and flow, diversion and abundance. The peatland is created and nurtured by water, and its presence was both visible and invisible as I scanned the horizon looking for the patterns I had seen in the photographs taken from a distant satellite. I thought of my own eye-level view as a kind of aerial imagery on a human scale; looking down, I saw a finely woven carpet of sedge and moss, bog rosemary and Labrador tea, red-lipped pitcher plants entwined with strands of small cranberry. All the composite parts of the peatland were there, surrounding me in time and space.

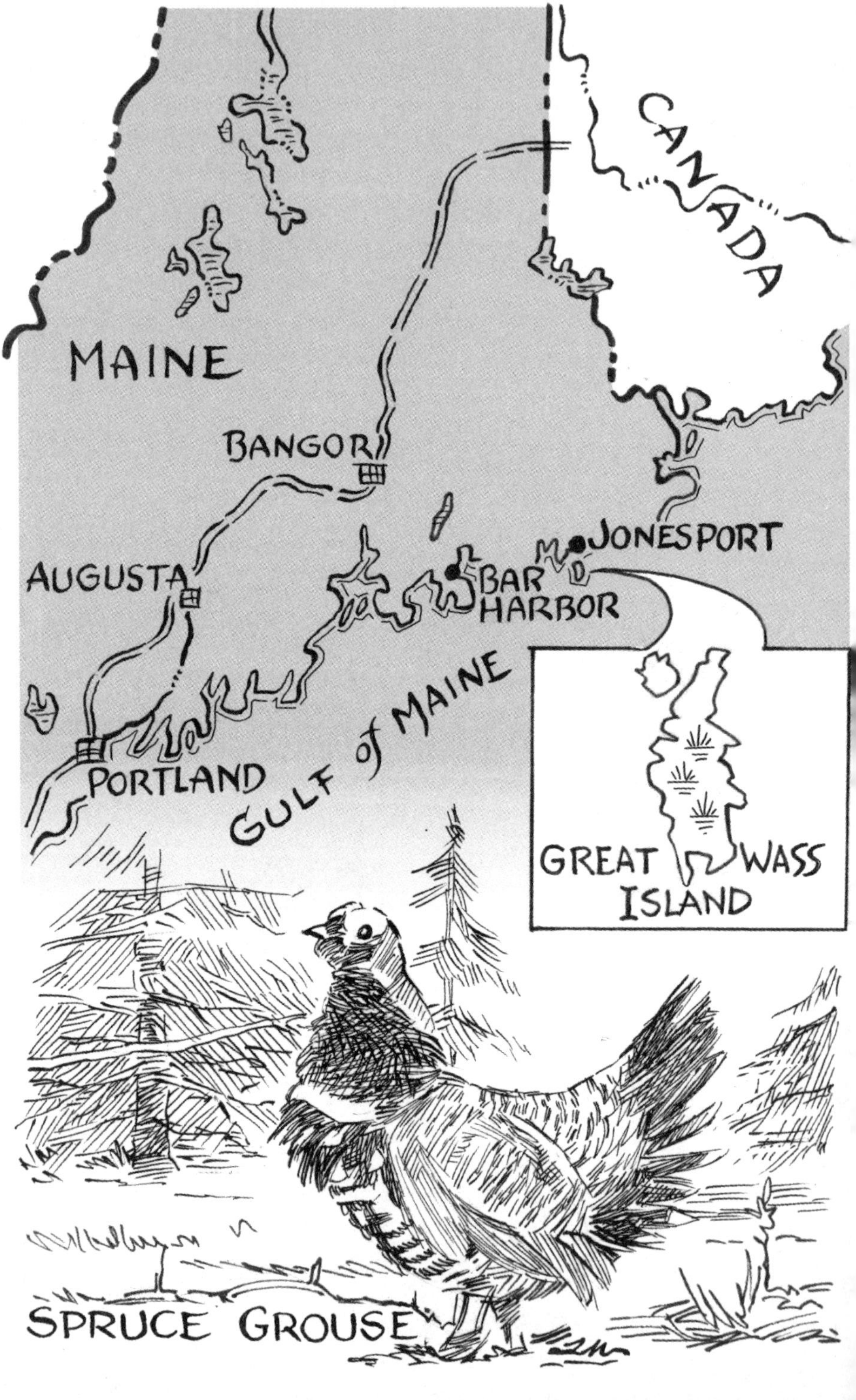

MAINE
CANADA
BANGOR
AUGUSTA
JONESPORT
BAR HARBOR
PORTLAND
GULF of MAINE
GREAT WASS ISLAND
SPRUCE GROUSE

TWO

Living on the Edge

Great Wass Island, Maine

Every living thing has its preferences. Food, shelter, climate—organisms seek out what they need, endure what they must. Animals have the advantage of mobility, allowing them to develop migratory strategies, traveling long or short distances to find a suitable niche to settle in, if only temporarily. Whether they roam far or near or not at all, animals have a range, a geographic limit to the places they inhabit. Plants move too, albeit on a slower timescale, and their ranges also can expand or contract. A species' home range is not fixed forever: Its boundaries are reshaped in sync with larger changes (like a warming planet), shifting north or south or edging higher or lower in altitude. Plants or animals may find themselves isolated in pockets of habitat left intact as the world changes around them.

Many northern peatlands trace their origins to the Pleistocene past, forming along the edges of retreating glaciers and expanding as the ice sheets disappeared. But peatlands can also be found outside the footprint of ice, even far to the south. Some of these isolated peatlands that arose in a cooler climate persist today, preserved under ecological conditions that support plants typically found in much colder latitudes. In the

Appalachians, for example, complex mountain topography has created "frost pockets" where cold, moist air sinks into a low, bowl-shaped valley, forming a refuge for boreal species common to the north. Naturalist Scott Weidensaul described these relict peatlands as "slices of the north embedded in the south." In West Virginia, the Cranberry Glades provides habitat for a number of songbirds found here at the southern edge of their range, including hermit and Swainson's thrushes, northern waterthrush, and mourning warblers.

Peatlands include bogs and fens—also known as mires, muskeg, or heath, depending on what part of the world you find them. The shades of difference between these varieties of peatlands relates to the source and quality of water that feeds them. Bogs are nourished by precipitation (rain and snow) and tend toward high acidity and low nutrients. Fens receive moisture from groundwater or surface streams as well as from the skies; the enriched water provides more available minerals and nutrients and, as a result, supports a more diverse range of plants. In simplistic terms, bogs are typically dominated by *Sphagnum* mosses, while fens are more often characterized by sedges.

Plants and animals that inhabit the world of peatlands are often living on the edge in more ways than one. Life in a peatland requires coping with extremes of moisture, acidity, and lack of nutrients. Some creatures, such as the wood frog, have remarkable survival skills; it can successfully reproduce in bog waters too acidic for most amphibians. Carnivorous plants have adapted to the lack of nutrients in peat soils by developing methods for capturing insects and absorbing their remains for nourishment. Peatlands can be harsh environments yet provide safe refuge to millions of migratory birds that travel to the boreal forest and tundra of Canada and Alaska every year to feast on the summer abundance of food and to nest in isolated peatlands. The Hudson and James Bay Lowlands, one of the largest contiguous peatland complexes in the world, supports breeding habitat for more than 130 bird species, including snow geese, sandhill cranes, palm warblers, and Hudsonian godwits, a shorebird famously known for its extraordinary migration route of nearly ten thousand miles from the Arctic north to the tip of South America.

Life on the edge has a literal meaning for peatlands that form on coastal margins. Maritime bogs are found on both Pacific and Atlantic shorelines, fed by the year-round abundance of moisture at the interface of land and sea. In the Pacific Northwest, bogs and fens are scattered along the coast of British Columbia, from Vancouver Island and the archipelago of Haida Gwaii up to southeast Alaska. Buffered from the surf by rocky beaches and narrow bands of dense conifer forest, these peatlands form a landscape of storm-twisted cedars, hemlocks, and pines underlain by a carpet of *Sphagnum* mosses.

Wet and wild as the rugged northwest coast is, it may have provided sanctuary for human travelers making their way into the New World. In the late Pleistocene, ice sheets that covered the northern half of the continent began to shrink away from the shore. Pockets of coastline that remained unglaciated served as refugia for plants and animals that were able to expand into newly available habitat as the ice retreated. According to a coastal migration hypothesis, people may have traveled along the Pacific coast from Asia to South America, covering each leg of the journey in relatively short distances. Making landfall at available beaches and bays would have given human migrants access to opportunities for wild game, as well as wood sources for repairing and building boats for onward travel.

On a remote island off the coast of British Columbia, evidence of these early travelers was discovered in 2014 in the form of footprints. Carbon dating of the wood fragments of shore pine pressed beneath the tracks showed the people who made these footprints were there sometime around thirteen thousand years ago—among the earliest known evidence of human presence in North America. Today, Calvert Island is a protected place, managed in part as a research reserve by the Hakai Institute. In one of the wettest regions of North America, fittingly called "hyper-maritime" climate, peatlands abound in a mosaic of bog, bog woodland, and bog forest. In some places the peat reaches twelve feet or more, holding the secret history of the island in its depths.

On the Eastern Seaboard of North America, the Atlantic coast holds peatland treasures too. Coastal bogs thrive in abundant precipitation and cool summers across eastern Canada's Maritime provinces, Newfoundland and Labrador, and Quebec. Though not as extensive as peatlands in the boreal north, bogs and fens dot the rugged shorelines and coastal plains of Maine, New York, Massachusetts, and New Jersey. Peatlands unique to the southeast, called pocosins, flourish in coastal plains of Virginia and the Carolinas. The Everglades basin of southern Florida is a vast subtropical peatland of fens and sawgrass marshes.

Coastal peatlands are reminders that the shoreline is not a static boundary. Some fifteen thousand years ago a large share of the world's freshwater was bound up in ice. Sea levels were more than three hundred feet lower than today, exposing broad stretches of the North American continental shelf. On the Atlantic coast, dry land extended a hundred miles or more to the east of present-day shorelines. Along the Pacific coast, the continental shelf is narrower, but the coast still would have been above water some thirty miles offshore of present-day shorelines. These coastal plains could have been occupied by plants, animals, and people whose presence has long since been submerged by the rising tides. Peatlands that cling to the margins of land today present archives of the past, but these too will one day be lost to the waves. Year by year, sea levels are rising; as the world warms, the waters of the ocean expand, edging farther inland. Every day, in six-hour cycles, the tide ebbs and flows.

Great Wass Island juts far out from the mainland, perched on the edge of the continental shelf into the Gulf of Maine, about thirty-five miles northeast of Acadia National Park. Along Maine's convoluted coast are a multitude of islands—three or four thousand, depending how you count them. Some of these lie close to the shoreline, like rafts still tethered to the mother ship. Many others are remote, accessible only by boat in rough seas, which is part of what makes them attractive to those who seek solitude. From the map, Great Wass Island looks like it is on its way to breaking into separate islets. But because of its proximity to the adjacent island of Beals, it is accessible by car via a thousand-foot bridge that connects the islands to the mainland.

The islands scattered along the coast of Maine were not always so isolated. Twenty-five thousand years ago, Great Wass and its neighboring islands were part of a connected land mass buried underneath a mile-deep layer of ice that covered all of Maine. The great Laurentide Ice Sheet stretched from the Arctic to New England and extended eastward, offshore from the present coastline to the edge of Georges Bank. As the ice thinned and retreated, the land of Down East Maine was revealed about fourteen thousand years ago. The regional reference to Down East Maine comes from more recent history: Nineteenth-century ships traveling in the summer months used the prevailing winds from the southwest to sail downwind toward the east, thus "down east."

Following my own prevailing winds, I had traveled to the northern- and easternmost part of the contiguous United States to explore peatlands that lie close to sea level. I arrived in Jonesport in mid-September, after the peak of summer visitors, and waited with a small knot of cars to cross the bridge to the islands of Beal and Great Wass. Following Black Duck Cove Road around the eastern shore, I crossed the three knobs of Great Wass, each separated by narrow isthmuses that looked like they might be prone to flooding at high tide. I wondered if I should have checked a tide log before setting out. As I continued south along the western edge of Great Wass, I passed Black Duck Cove and found the entrance to a preserve managed by The Nature Conservancy, which acquired the property in 1978. The preserve encompasses more than fifteen hundred acres—about 90 percent of the southern lobe of Great Wass Island—created to protect the unique forest and peatland ecosystems.

Dressed in layers for the coastal chill, I started my solo hike on Little Cape Point Trail, which crosses the island west to east, ending at Cape Cove in just a little over two miles. Such a short distance seemed like a brief glance into the heart of the island's wilderness, but I spent most of the day moving slowly and stopping often. Each bend in the trail, rise over a granite dome, or climb across a tangle of tree roots offered a detailed view of the forest interior. There were no great peaks or precipices, but stony outcroppings fringed with pines and blanketed with plush mosses. Where the forest opened to a ledge, I clambered to the top of a boulder and perched on a flat spot sheltered by jack pines, imagining a giant map of North America with an arrow labeled "you are here" pointing to the spot on this outermost speck of land.

The peatland on Great Wass Island represents a type of raised bog, found in the coastal band from the southern tip of Mount Desert Island to West Quoddy Head, known as a coastal plateau bog. Instead of forming a dome, as typically found in inland raised bogs, the bog slope develops into a level, flattened surface, hence the name "plateau." Where other raised bogs resemble an unmade bed, with a rumpled surface of hummocks and hollows, the coastal plateau bog creates a wide plain, nearly flat or gently sloped and dominated by rusty peatmoss, forming a velvety cushion of *Sphagnum*. The central plateau is generally treeless and dense with black crowberry, abundant here but rarely found inland, and cloudberry, also known as baked-apple berry, a thornless relative of the raspberry and blackberry.

The presence of jack pines is one of the distinctive features of the Great Wass peatlands; though a fairly common species farther north, jack pines occur here at the southern edge of their range in Maine. On Great Wass, jack pines can be found on both rocky outcrops and in the coastal plateau bogs, habitats with very different growing conditions ranging from thin, dry mineral soils to deeply saturated peat. Jack pines are one of several pine species with closed cones; an adaptation to wildfire, the tight-knit scales open only when exposed to high temperatures, scattering the seeds onto bare soil enriched by ash and open to sunlight. The pines on Great Wass, however, present something of a mystery. The occurrence of jack pines in the coastal plateau bogs appears to be a recent trend, and their spread does not seem to be related to fire. Research conducted by Andrew Barton and Daniel Grenier found no history of fire on the island in the past century; their study of individual jack pines on Great Wass showed trees with and without the resin that keeps the scales and seeds sealed tight. Stands of pines are reproducing on both rocky outcrops and coastal plateau bogs. Something in the peat must agree with them: Jack pines growing in bogs were larger and had fewer dead limbs. The encroachment of jack pines is changing the structure and appearance of the peatlands on Great Wass. Aerial photos from 1940 to 1996 show that the treeless areas of plateau bogs have shrunk by almost half as new trees—mostly jack pines—have taken root, literally. The recent history of colonization is evidenced by the ages of these trees, with individual trees on the rocky outcrops dating back to the early 1800s, while the oldest trees found in bog habitat date to the 1890s.

There is some evidence of pines invading peatlands in parts of Europe and Canada, possibly in response to declining surface moisture in bogs. Even small changes in the depth of the water table can create conditions more or less favorable to tree growth. Whether the changes are driven by increasing temperatures or decreasing precipitation is uncertain, and how those changes might be amplified by climate change is also unknown. The Gulf of Maine is experiencing rapid warming in sea temperatures, both at the surface and in deeper water, which in turn affects ocean currents that pull cold, nutrient-rich waters from the northern Labrador Current into the Gulf of Maine. These deep-water currents have been weakening and warming in recent years; at the same time, the Gulf Stream is shifting northward. The influx of warmer waters has dramatic impacts on the marine food chain, triggering huge declines in the populations of copepods, an essential food source for a range of sea life from cod and herring to the Atlantic right whale. Accelerated warming has a wide influence across the Northern Hemisphere: As arctic temperatures increase, the jet stream slows, causing weather patterns to get stuck in place for days or weeks at a time. A heat wave, even in relative terms, can shut down the conditions that keep coastal Maine bathed in cool fog, leaving coastal plateau peatlands high and dry.

Climate plays an essential role in bog formation, and here in Maine I had found true bogs—peatlands whose source of water comes only from the sky. The wet coastal climate found in the northeastern United States and Canadian Maritime provinces provides the optimum conditions for the formation of raised bogs, which are peatlands that increase in elevation as layers of peat accumulate over time. Raised bogs may form mound- or dome-shaped landforms, creating a concave surface over the depression in which the bog initially formed. As the surface of the bog rises, the water held in the peat layers becomes elevated above the water table of the surrounding landscape. Due to the isolation of the water table, the raised bog is fed only by water from the atmosphere: rain, snow, and fog. Where the available moisture is a surplus (more than what is lost through evaporation and plant respiration), raised peatlands can continue to grow upward and outward, spreading both vertically and horizontally.

Along the coast of northern Maine, the maritime climate is famous for high rainfall and persistent fog and cloud cover. Moderated by ocean air currents, this narrow rim of the continent is warmer in winter and cooler and moister in summer than the forests of interior Maine. Even the average annual precipitation of around fifty inches may be an underestimate: Vegetation can intercept moisture from fog, and the steady drip of water adds to the water content received from rainfall. The ocean air creates a consistently cool, moist environment and provides some nutrients, stirred up in the surf and rendered airborne.

Up and down the Maine coast, I explored peatlands from West Quoddy Head, on the easternmost tip of land in the United States, to Corea Heath on the Schoodic Peninsula, through the black spruce bogs of Basin Preserve on the Phippsburg Peninsula. Each one has its own unique history, but all were once bare ground after the retreat of the ice sheets. Seeds blew in, plants took root, pollen and leaves floated on the surface of shallow ponds. Over time, sedges and tundra grasses made room for dwarf alders and willow, followed by pioneer tree species—each contributing its leaves, seeds, pollen, and wood to the layers of organic matter that transformed the landscape from rock and gravel to weathered soils that could absorb water.

Across Maine, forests have responded to a variety of changes in climate, both large-scale and local, over the millennia since the last glaciers retreated. As temperatures rose, tundra gave way to spruce-fir forests, shifting to pines and oaks when conditions were drier, then to beech and hemlock when the climate became moister. The extensive forests of spruce and fir found in Maine today returned a mere fifteen hundred years ago when temperatures cooled again. In fewer than ten thousand years, Maine has evolved from a bare, rocky landscape to a lush expanse of forests and wetlands. Great Wass Island is a remnant of this history, supporting plants and animals from alpine, boreal, and arctic environments.

Biogeography, the study of where living things are found and why, is a subject that has fascinated naturalists, ecologists, and explorers for centuries. Charles Darwin made detailed observations of the differences between finches found on each of the Galapagos Islands during his voyage on the *Beagle*. Alexander von Humboldt, in his travels in South America, recorded shifts in plant communities at different altitudes in the Andes and noticed similar changes as he moved north or south from the equator. Many peatlands provide the ecological conditions for plants typically found in much colder latitudes. In his book *The Changing Nature of the Maine Woods*, Andrew Barton wrote that many tree species widely found in Canada, including balsam fir, jack pine, and white spruce, reach the southern boundary of their range in Maine. Coastal peatlands like Great Wass serve as a safe harbor for boreal refugees, offering shelter in the cool climate and maritime moisture.

Changes in climate trigger complex shifts in vegetation, reshaping the geographic footprint of plant communities and altering the mix of species. Today, ecosystems are on the move, and rapidly warming temperatures are affecting boreal forests throughout their range. Studies of satellite data show that boreal forest habitat is migrating northward, as the northern edge of the forest expands and the southern edge retreats. These ecological shifts have occurred in the past, but not at the current rates of change in global temperatures. Scientists worry that, if the southern edge of forest range moves northward at a faster pace than the northern boundary, the boreal forest will contract. And as boreal forest shrinks, so too does habitat for dozens of animal species that depend on the food, shelter, and nesting habitat that the forest provides.

As I meandered along the path through the forest depths, I stepped through a maze of running club moss—well-named, as it had the appearance of racing across the forest floor. A member of the ancient family of Lycopodiaceae, these plants are fern allies: evergreens with leafy horizontal stems ornamented with spore-bearing clubs that grow upright like pale green candelabra. I bent down for a closer look, and when I stood up again, a trio of spruce grouse was looking at me with mild alarm. Perfectly still, the birds blend into the forest floor so well that I could have easily overlooked them, if not for the cardinal-red eyebrow that gives them a look of perpetual surprise. Spruce grouse are shy birds that spend most of their time on the ground, traveling on foot in search of their primary diet of conifer needles. Relatively common across the boreal forests of Canada, these birds were on the southern edge of their habitat range. Spruce grouse are not migratory, though they may travel short distances between summer and winter feeding areas. As the grouse and I eyed one another, I thought of the birds scuffling along in the understory of the dark woods, heading north. For the moment, they seemed quite at home in the deep woods of Great Wass.

PERU
ANDES MOUNTAINS
MARCAPOMACOCHA
SANTA EULALIA RIVER
LIMA
PACIFIC OCEAN

THREE

High and Low

Marcapomacocha, Peru

Seek and you shall find. Looking at a world map produced by the Global Peatlands Initiative, a wide swath of dark red (the color used to depict peatland distribution) sweeps east-west across Russia, Canada, and Alaska, grabbing the viewer's eye. About 80 percent of the world's peatlands are in northern temperate or cold climates. But let your gaze wander south: Hot spots of peat are visible in Asia, Africa, and South America. Even in the winterless warmth of the tropics, peatlands can be found in continental interiors and coastal margins, from tropical lowlands to high-elevation mountains.

Peatlands can be remote and easily overlooked, but they are of intense interest to scientists, geographers, and environmental policymakers. Research on peatlands has been going on for decades, led by universities and, increasingly, international agencies focused on conservation and climate change. In Germany, the University of Greifswald, founded in 1456, developed a research program on peatland science as early as 1820. In the 1990s, the university established a working group on peatland studies and paleoecology, followed by the creation of the Greifswald Mire Centre in 2015. One of their major initiatives is coordinating an international network of scientists to maintain a Global Peatland Database—a work in progress that collects and synthesizes peatland data on the location and condition of peatlands worldwide—and which informs a series of maps depicting the geographic diversity of peatland.

Global estimates of peatlands in the tropics and subtropics vary widely, in part because the more scientists look, the more they discover. One paper in 2011 estimated the total area of tropical peatland to be 441,000 square kilometers (almost twice the size of Minnesota), the majority of which lay in Indonesia and Malaysia. Then, in 2012, researchers from the University of Leeds and University College London found peat deposits that made news headlines. In the Cuvette Centrale region of the Republic of Congo, scientists found peatlands of roughly 150,000 square kilometers, about twice the size of Ireland. Another paper, published in 2017, proposed a revised estimate of 1.7 million square kilometers of tropical and subtropical peatlands, more than three times the 2011 assessment.

Mapping the extent of peatland is challenging for several reasons. Aerial and satellite images and remote-sensing data can be incredibly valuable for tracing peatlands in distant places. Looking at the peatland map, you can see why these technologies are necessary for exploring the inaccessible corners of the world where ground-truthing is limited. Many tropical peatland sites are not only difficult to reach; the waterlogged ground makes fieldwork precarious. Remote sensing provides sophisticated tools that can indicate where peatlands may be. Computer modeling and use of proxy data, such as vegetation types or topography, can also reveal hidden patterns in peatland distribution. But in tropical regions with dense vegetation, it is not always clear which areas are peat-accumulating and which are not. Thus, the maps change, and the estimates change with them. Even where the boundaries of a peatland area can be roughly sketched out, there is the problem of estimating the depth of peat—an essential factor in quantifying the volume of the peat deposit and amount of carbon it holds. Measurements like these may seem esoteric, but they play an important part in figuring out the role of tropical peatlands in the global carbon cycle. How much carbon is absorbed by plants and stored in soils versus how much is emitted to the atmosphere? The numbers are integral parts of a bigger climate equation.

Brazil boasts the largest total area of peatlands in South America, but peat is found throughout the Amazon and upper reaches of its tributary rivers. Scientists have made considerable efforts to map peatlands in Peru, and these remain some of the best-studied sites. In 2008, a team of ecologists began field research in the Pastaza-Marañón Foreland Basin of northwestern Peru, the most extensive peatland known in the Amazon region. Peatlands here cover about a third of the lowland basin which formed during the geologic uplift that created the Andes mountain ranges. High rainfall and frequent flooding offer the conditions that support peat formation. The ecosystem types found here are unlike the peatlands of the north. Tropical peat is produced mainly from trees, rather than mosses. Some tree species contain chemical compounds that inhibit microbial activity, slowing down decomposition and aiding the formation of peat. Palm swamp forest is dominated by aguaje, a palm that produces tasty fruit, an important food source for people and for native animals like the tapir. Peatland pole forest forms an almost impenetrable thicket of thin-stemmed trees, underlain by deep reservoirs of peat. Researchers sampling aboveground and belowground carbon consider this forest type to be the most carbon-dense ecosystem yet found in Amazonia.

Peatlands form a fringe along the Caribbean coastal shores, from the Yucatan Peninsula to Panama, underlying mangrove thickets and *Raphia* palm swamps. Farther south are the temperate peatlands of Patagonia and Tierra del Fuego. In this vast region, lying between 36 and 56 degrees south latitude, peatland ecosystems vary with the rainfall, which ranges from more than one hundred inches per year on the Pacific coast of Chile to less than twelve inches on the drier steppes lying in the windy rain shadow of the Andes. Along the gradient of wet to dry, peatland vegetation changes from deep hummocky bogs dominated by the aptly named Magellan's peatmoss to windswept fens, or vegas, covered with sedges and grasses.

Perhaps the most remote peatlands in South America are those found in the subtropical mountains, where cushion bogs can be found at elevations up to fifteen thousand feet. Mountain landscapes are physically dramatic and ecologically dynamic. Powerful forces lift and grind slabs of rock. Water falls as rain or snow, freezing in cracks and scouring boulders into cobblestones. Sun and wind pull moisture from the thin soil, subjecting them to persistent erosion—not a likely scene for the creation of peatlands. Yet here and there, scattered in small pockets, are peatlands kept moist by the year-round supply of precious groundwater. They require enough moisture and sufficient plant productivity for organic matter to accumulate, a delicate balance of conditions that must persist, unbroken, for the plant material to become peat. Mountain peatlands are rare because the conditions needed to sustain them are rare.

A good map or a knowledgeable guide may help you find peatlands in the wildness of the southern latitudes. But even the best maps are only a set of clues—sometimes you just have to go looking.

Traveling southward down the coast of Peru, the landscape seemed an endless canvas of monochrome sand and rock. The coastal desert extends all the way to Chile where it joins the Atacama Desert, considered one of the driest places on the planet.

As our van followed the Pan-American Highway parallel to the shoreline, the blue Pacific sparkled brightly to the west, sharpening the contrast to the parched earth. I was traveling with a small group of birders (four Brits, my husband, and myself) led by our Peruvian guide José Antonio. At the wheel was our driver, also named José Antonio, who we would soon learn had nerves of steel in navigating narrow mountain roads.

A shock of green farmland appeared wherever a river descended from the mountains. Irrigation in the coastal region is essential to agriculture, supporting food production for Peru's population of more than thirty-two million people. Glacial meltwater from the high Andes mountain range is the lifeblood supporting irrigated cropland, making Peru the leading exporter of asparagus worldwide and a major producer of grapes and avocados. The arid western slope of the Andes is part of what makes Peru so diverse ecologically; the country's varied geography includes desert, high mountains, and Amazon rainforest. As a result, Peru boasts one of the highest rates of biodiversity in the world, with more than eighteen hundred bird species—more than North America and Europe combined.

As we turned inland, our ascent into the Peruvian highlands followed the Santa Eulalia River. The broad slopes of the coastal desert gave way to steep canyon walls dropping into the riverbed of cobbled stone. The mountain roads appeared to be chipped by hand into the vertical landscape, winding steadily upward as the distant river below became a thin blue-gray line brushed with frothy white where the water broke into rapids.

The sky changed to a clear pale blue punctuated with distinct cloud shapes. On the coast, and for much of the way up into the highlands, the sky was weighted with a heavy cover of ocean fog darkened by truck exhaust. The persistent cloud layer is largely due to the Humboldt Current along the coast of Peru; its cold waters create the desert climate, as cool air holds little moisture that quickly turns to fog, rather than rain, as it encounters the warmer land surface. This interface of coastal air and land felt familiar; the legendary fog of San Francisco, my former home ground, is formed under the same conditions.

We stopped for the night in the village of San Lorenzo de Huachupampa, a stepping-off place to our destination: the high-elevation peatlands of the central Andes. From here the road became narrower and steeper, climbing more than six thousand feet in just twenty miles and crossing a high unnamed pass at close to sixteen thousand feet. As we gained altitude, the afternoon turned cloudy and chilly, with rain spitting in brief intervals. The terrain widened to a broad valley flanked by forbidding peaks, their jagged edges muted by clouds and rain. Below us the scene was a sweeping vista of green in a wide, U-shaped valley ringed by high ridges capped with snow and glacial ice. A large, shallow lake lay still as a dark mirror encircled by a fringe of mossy green.

The surrounding slopes were trimmed with thick tufts of sedges or grass, part of the complex of plant communities that plays a critical role in the local hydrology, storing and regulating water flow above- and belowground. Tall blond bunchgrasses, called *ichu,* are the natural grazing diet for llamas and alpacas, the domesticated relatives of native guanacos and vicuñas. This is the Andean *puna,* a grassland habitat that encompasses a swath of the Andes range through Peru, Bolivia, Chile, and Argentina. Lying above the tree line and below the snow line, roughly thirteen to sixteen thousand feet above sea level, the puna of central Peru is a covered by grasses, sedges, and rushes. Rainfall here is significantly higher than on the coast, ranging from twenty to thirty-five inches a year—a dramatic difference from Lima, which often receives no measurable rainfall except in years with El Niño conditions. The relative abundance of precipitation, though, belies the extremity of the climate. Rainfall is seasonal, with long dry spells and frequent droughts; at these altitudes, the humidity is low and intensity of solar radiation is high.

The weather pattern of the Andean highlands can create all four seasons in a day: The daily range of high to low temperatures can vary as much as 60 degrees Fahrenheit, much greater than the seasonal variation in temperature. Frosts are common, as nighttime temperatures fall below freezing most nights. The severe temperature swings not only limit what plants can survive in the puna, they also limit the process of decomposition. As plants die and break down slowly, a thick layer of organic matter accumulates, holding water that would otherwise be lost in the thin dry air. This combination of weather, water, and plants supplies the ingredients for the unique wetlands of the puna.

In Peru, *bofedales* is the regional name for these high-altitude wetlands. There is no exact English translation for the word, but these wetland communities are often (but not always) peatlands, integrated in the puna grassland ecosystem like pieces of a mosaic. The landscape is thick with dense clusters of low-growing plants with waxy leaves arrayed in geometric patterns. Many of the plants found here have adaptations similar to plants in desert habitats: *Distichia* and *Plantago* are just two of the plant genera that grow tightly together on the surface, forming an almost impenetrable cover of low vegetation that holds in moisture and reduces evaporation. Unlike the peatlands in the northern hemisphere, *Sphagnum* mosses are not a common component in Andean peatlands.

I stood at the edge of the road, sharp gravel crunching underfoot, taking in the peatland panorama. As if to provide a caption to the picture, a pair of Andean geese stood on the gentle slope, their pink bills and orange feet visible at a distance. Like any wetland in an otherwise arid environment, bofedales are rich ecosystems for wildlife, especially birds. Many of the bird species found here are considered threatened, and all are dependent to some degree on the peatlands as a source of food, water, and nesting habitat. After our long trek up the Santa Eulalia Valley, we reached the highlands, where we found many of the iconic birds of the bofedales and puna grasslands: Andean gull, crested duck, Andean lapwing, puna snipe, giant coot, Andean flicker, and white-bellied cinclodes. Most of the birds here are residents, not casual visitors or migrants. This stark and seemingly inhospitable landscape offers enough food and relative safety from predators to support a collection of alpine bird species found only at these high elevations.

Small streams wound through the peat, with pools of surface water here and there reflecting the silvery sky. The impression was of robust greenness—visible proof of life in these rocky highlands. No trees were in sight and few shrubs, though many of these spindly bushes were in flower. Even the giant hummingbird, found up to fifteen thousand feet, can find sustenance here. Snaking switchbacks descended toward a crossroads, where the road that leads to Marcapomacocha crosses a railroad line that appears out of the blue, its terminus at the foot of a quarry. The peatlands nearby were reported to be a good spot for seeing the diademed sandpiper-plover, one of the rare birds found only in high-elevation peatlands. After hours of traveling on rough roads through remote mountain terrain, I felt a sense of disappointment that such a rare bird might live on the doorstep of a large-scale mining operation. As it happened, the bird was not to be found, so we retraced the winding road to a wide, spreading wetland dotted with green mounds of cushion plants that make up the bofedale wetland. The stillness of the place was profound; between the low cloud cover and the wet hummocky earth, nothing stirred. Then, a slight flutter caught our attention. Camouflaged against the tweed of mossy green were two, then three, of these exquisite shorebirds. The diadem refers to the white stripe above the eye that encircles the head like a tiara; with its delicately barred breast and a chestnut mantle, the diademed sandpiper-plover has the plumage of bird royalty.

While my companions were keeping their attention fixed to binoculars and spotting scopes, I stopped to rest my eyes on the ground. The pattern of plants in this watery world demanded a closer look. On my hands and knees, I could see the detailed composition of individual plants, growing tightly together to form a dense, almost impenetrable layer of thick leaves. Because they create a unique microtopography of mounded plant clusters, these bofedales are sometimes called "cushion bogs," a term also used to describe peatlands in New Zealand and Australia. Underneath my feet and all around me was a tightly knitted carpet of a tiny, ground-hugging plant called *Plantago tubulosa.* Higher up the mountain road, the bofedales were rich with *Distichia,* a member of the plant family of rushes (Juncaceae). These various plant communities often grow in close association, more of a patchwork than distinctly defined habitats.

Some bofedales are intersected by streams, while in other areas the peatlands form a broad meadow. Knowing the sources of water that support peatlands is important to understanding the ecology of these wetlands. Because bofedales are fed partly by groundwater, mostly through springs and snowmelt, they are technically classified as fens, not bogs. These wetlands serve an essential function for both people and wildlife by regulating water supply. High-elevation peatlands act as enormous sponges, storing and releasing water through underground flow. Precipitation in the high Andes is dramatically variable: Cold, dry winters are relieved by intense rainfall in the short summer season. Water from snow and glacial melt travels through underlying rock, emerging through springs and seeps. Much of this water would be lost to wind and sun if it were not absorbed in the thick peat layers of the bofedales. This stored water connects to a larger hydrological network that delivers water to streams that feed into rivers flowing down the western slope, sustaining the water supply to Peru's coastal cities and farms. The timing and volume of water flow from the Andes is also critical to the production of hydroelectric power, which provides about half of the electricity in Peru.

Traveling up the highway toward Ticlio Pass, we made our last and highest stop at fifteen thousand feet. I felt the dropping temperature in my fingers and toes. In early morning the surface of the bofedale glistened with frost. The thin, icy air was sharp with each inhaled breath. Despite the cold, I could see that the thin coating of ice would be melting by midmorning and absorbed into the peat. Looking up at the frozen caps surrounding the shallow, green bowl of the peatland, I tried to imagine what the extent of alpine glaciers might have been a decade, or a century, past. Throughout the tropical Andes, climate change is driving increasing temperatures that could dramatically change the availability of precious water in this ecosystem. Many scientists recognize that rising temperatures have affected high elevations more directly than lowland habitats. The Peruvian Andes hold 70 percent of the world's tropical glaciers and, like glaciers in other parts of the world, these are shrinking rapidly. By some measures, Peru's glaciers have diminished in surface area by 40 percent in the past fifty years.

Water security is not only a benefit to downstream communities; it is also essential to the pastoralist culture of the high Andes, where grazing animals have been a traditional livelihood since pre-Hispanic times. For centuries, people have modified the local hydrology to support and expand the year-round supply of water in bofedales that serve as pasture for alpacas and llamas. Bofedales are often found near springs, where subsurface flow of water from glacier or snowmelt supplies a year-round source of moisture to support the wetland vegetation. Even these groundwater sources can be inconsistent, and so, over many generations, herders have constructed networks of channels to ensure a constant influx of water to sustain the grazing lands on which they depend. While livestock grazing has a long history in the puna region, changes in practices can damage the wetland ecosystems. Cattle and horses, introduced during the Spanish conquest, require larger amounts of forage, and their heavier body weight damages vegetation. Overgrazing or soil compaction from too many animals threatens the stability of these wetlands, and the extreme climate conditions make recovery of any disturbance to peatlands very slow.

I watched a few dozen llamas grazing on a broad slope between Ticlio Pass and a distant arc of mountains. At the base of a rocky outcrop was a small hut, a crooked box built from sheets of rusty corrugated metal—presumably a shelter for whoever tended the animals. A cold and lonely outpost, and yet I could imagine the wonder of awakening to a glittering clear morning on the top of the world. Excited voices caught my attention, and I turned in time to see the elusive birds my companions had been seeking. The puna tinamou is a quail-shaped bird of the high Andes, well camouflaged to blend into the rocky puna grasslands and patches of cushion plants. Finding this bird took patience and sharp hearing: Their soft, flute-like call can be tossed on the wind like a ventriloquist throwing his voice. The birds shuffled through clumps of pale gold bunchgrasses and across a dense carpet of green, the thick overcoat of peat layers hidden beneath. At this altitude, I had to stop to catch my breath.

PART II

water

NY
ALLEGHENY MTS
SCRANTON
MOUNTAINS
POCONO MTS
TANNERSVILLE CRANBERRY BOG
APPALACHIAN
BLUE MT.
ALLENTOWN
HARRISBURG
PHILADELPHIA
PENNSYLVANIA
MD
DE
NJ
= OTHER BOGS
PITCHER PLANT

FOUR

Water Worlds

Tannersville Cranberry Bog, Pennsylvania

Looking for peatlands requires curiosity and an eye for detail. Still, it can be a challenge to recognize a bog when you see one. Unlike a grove of giant sequoias or a saguaro cactus desert, peatlands have no singular characteristic in structure or vegetation. They may be shrubby or forested, covered in dense sedges or hummocky meadows of moss. I walked along trails where a peatland lay just outside my view, past a thorny thicket or a stand of trees, while I was completely oblivious to its presence. It was humbling to discover that I had no natural gift for finding peatlands when I wanted so much to discover their obscure beauty. I learned to see them by looking through different lenses—those of the geographer, the ecologist, and the botanist.

All peatlands are wetlands. There are various ways to categorize wetlands, one of which recognizes three basic groups: tidal, riverine, and palustrine. Tidal and riverine, as the names suggest, refer to coastal areas and wetlands connected to flowing water. Peatlands fall into the category of palustrine wetlands, along with freshwater ponds and lakes. The margin of a pond has a distinct shoreline, though it may be blurred by a fringe of cattails or a thicket of willows. There is an edge to the surface water, a place where a person could stand with one foot on dry land and one foot in the water. Peatlands differ from lakes and ponds in that they hold reservoirs of water that are largely contained in their saturated soils, hidden underground. The water is just below the surface—poke a finger into the springy cover of moss and you'll find moisture. Many peatlands do have areas of open water that appear when groundwater rises to the surface, often during a rainy season or after spring snowmelt in northern peatlands. Some peatlands form in lakebeds; it may be impossible to know if a lake bottom is composed of peat or mud just by looking at it.

Common names for peatlands vary across the map, but these can sometimes be misleading. Some places called a marsh or swamp may in fact be a bog. And some places named bog are not truly bogs, but wetlands of some other variety. A peatland that receives water only from the sky—rain, snow, fog—is considered a true bog. These rain-fed, or *ombrotrophic,* peatlands are exceptionally low in nutrients. Many peatlands, though, form in places where water can reach them from streams, springs, or groundwater. These are described as *minerotrophic* peatlands or, more commonly, fens. The inflow of water enriches the habitat as it imports organic matter from the surrounding uplands and valuable minerals collected as the water moves through pores in the soil or underlying bedrock. Like adding fertilizer to a garden bed, the benefit of additional water sources results in a more tolerable environment for a wider range of plant species. Peatlands range from poor bogs to rich fens, classifications of wealth being relative to the local availability of nutrients and minerals. Sometimes the differences are visible, evidenced by the plant species that are ecological indicators of bogs and fens.

The landscape and its history, the sources of water and nutrients: These are the patterns that the geographer and the ecologist examine to understand the nature of peatlands. A geographer reads topographic and geological signs to understand the origin and character of a peatland. She sees a shallow basin or a narrow gap on the lee side of a mountain slope. The unseen traces of water courses in the soil beneath her feet. The enduring imprint of slow-moving sheets of ice. The mineral world creates the physical structure and chemistry for peatlands to form. Climate and latitude add their voices to the creation story. An ecologist looks at a peatland from another perspective, as a natural system defined by water, nutrients, and organisms. The source of water is central to the peatland's identity—the essence of the living world you will find in it. In one place, the ecologist finds peatlands thick with black spruce forest or peppered with ghostly tamaracks. In another, she sees deep moss lawns encircled by impenetrable shrublands stretching to the horizon. What survives and what thrives in these water worlds is a tale of adaptation.

A botanist's view leads us closer, introducing us to the family members that live in these unique wetlands. The plants that thrive here are not passive residents, just tolerating the extreme conditions of saturated soils and limited nutrients. Many of them are ecosystem builders, designers of their environment. Plants, like people, need food, air, and water to survive. Living in a waterlogged environment, these necessities are not always easy to come by. The challenges of peatland ecosystems are daunting for many plant species: limited nutrients, low oxygen, high acidity. Yet evolution provides plants with mechanisms for innovation and adaptation, giving some plants a competitive advantage in surviving these limitations—and these species not only survive, they thrive.

In a light summer rain, the drowsy sound of water dripping from leaves and the soft swish of nylon rain gear was amplified in the hush of the forest. Not discouraged by the sodden sky,

I considered this the perfect weather for exploring a peatland: an immersion experience of life in a water world. I lingered by the opening of a forest path that led into Tannersville Cranberry Bog Preserve, a kettlehole bog nestled between dips and swales of the Pocono Mountains. Our guide from Monroe County Conservation District's Kettle Creek Environmental Education Center pulled up in a truck and hopped out to greet my husband and me, the only two guests who turned up for a scheduled walk. The bog is a fragile place, and although a floating boardwalk enables visitors to tread lightly, access is limited to guided visits. Cheerful despite the rain, the guide radiated enthusiasm for the preserve's unique habitat and its significance as a protected area. We entered the forest, following a scant trail that climbed over a gentle rise that our guide referred to as "the ridge." The topography is subtle but reveals part of the origin story of the bog.

Ten thousand years ago, the irresistible force of moving ice met an immovable object near the base of a small mountain in northeastern Pennsylvania. A bump of bedrock shale was enough to stop a glacier in its tracks, and as glacial action scoured out a depression at the base of that rocky obstacle, it created a dip in the topography that set the stage for formation of a certain kind of peatland. Glaciers are untidy guests, leaving chunks of ice and rock in their wake. The landscape left behind is dotted with divots that fill with water as the ice melts. These flooded pockets can persist for centuries or, over time, become acidic wetlands known as kettlehole bogs. Kettleholes generally form level bogs, often with no streams flowing in or out. A kettlehole can be easily hidden as a quiet glade where the water is held in a pocket of saturated peat that slowly accumulates, century by century, for millennia.

Although it lies adjacent to Cranberry Creek, Tannersville Bog is a rain-fed system. The water in the bog is highly acidic, with a pH of 3.2 to 3.3, about the same as grapefruit juice. Cranberry Creek is less acidic with a pH around 5, influenced not by the bog but by the creek headwaters that flow from a nearby maple swamp. Water levels in the bog can fluctuate quickly; after a significant rainfall the water can rise several inches. Only occasionally does the creek run high enough to spill over into the bog. Seasonally, the water tends to be highest in spring and lowest in late summer, unless a late-season tropical storm brings heavy rainfall. In August 1955, back-to-back hurricanes, named Connie and Diane, unloaded more than twenty inches of rainfall on the Poconos in a matter of days, producing some of the worst flooding in the region's history. Across eastern Pennsylvania, bridges and dams were damaged or destroyed—except along Cranberry Creek. Downstream from Tannersville Cranberry Bog, road bridges remained intact. The bog had provided a measure of flood protection by absorbing and slowing water flow. Flooding events can have a dramatic effect on bogs in the short term, with an infusion of nutrients and a sudden change in water chemistry, but peatland conditions prevail in the long run. Any upland plants or seeds swept into the peatland will have to endure the persistent saturation, acidity, and lack of nutrients to become established.

On the forest path, the rain continued as we neared the bog, but there was no threat of flooding. The peatland embraces all the water the skies can offer. We traversed a transition zone between the forest and the bog, and then stepped unsteadily onto a boardwalk. The wooden planks teetered at odd angles, a reflection of age (the boardwalk was first installed in the 1980s) and the construction method: The slats are attached to plastic barrels that allow the boardwalk to rise and fall with changing water levels. The tread was slippery, as the wood has worn to a water-softened polish. Preserve staff had nailed on strips of carpet remnants to provide a bit of friction, but each footstep required nimble balance. With only a few places in the bog exposing small windows of open water, the vegetation layers in the bog were lush and complex. Thickets of highbush blueberry, bog laurel, and leatherleaf reached eye level. The calla lilies and blue flag iris were blooming everywhere, and the ruby-red flowers of northern pitcher plants rose up above the moss on slender stalks.

I knelt down next to a lush patch of pitcher plants, crowded together like a nest of baby birds with open beaks. Many of the pitchers held rainwater in which I could see the reflection of the clouded sky. Nutrient-poor conditions in a kettlehole bog make it inhospitable for many plant species. Those that do well here are adapted to the limited menu the bog offers, and some of them have developed ingenious ways to eke out a living. Pitcher plants nestle deep in the moss layer, a well-disguised trap for wandering insects to become dietary supplements for these carnivorous plants. Pitcher plants grew in clusters as large as my fist, with smooth, waxy leaves modified into upright tubes that present an open invitation for a closer look. Satiny, green trumpets with rich purple-red veins, each pitcher seems to have its own unique pattern, some bright emerald green with spidery crimson veins, others a deep cherry-red dappled with chartreuse. Combined with powerful visual cues for attracting insects is the lure of copious amounts of sweet nectar, a blend of color and fragrance that draws prey into the pitfall traps.

The slippery slope begins at the pitcher's opening. Northern pitcher plants have an upright hood formed by the wavy edge of the upper leaf. The underside of this leaf is textured with hair-like structures that point downward into the pitcher. Insects investigating this opening will find it all too easy to slide farther into the well but almost impossible to climb out. Nectar glands that line the inside of the tube exude sugar-rich substances that entice and beguile the hapless insect. Pointed skyward, the pitcher plant tube is an effective container for capturing rainfall, and this creates the ultimate hazard for an unlucky insect. At the bottom of the well, the creature drowns in a pool of water mixed with digestive enzymes and bacteria, and there begins the slow process of decomposition and absorption. In other species of pitcher plant, the leafy hood covers the opening of the pitcher, which prevents too much rain from accumulating and diluting the enzyme bath needed for dissolving and digesting prey. Insects are not the only ones to fall into the abyss—pitcher plants are known to trap spiders, slugs, and even small amphibians—thus these plants are considered carnivorous rather than strictly insectivorous.

In a small thicket of pitcher plants, a dozen or more burgundy red flowers hung from the shepherd's crook of tall stems. The pitcher plant flower is an intricate design, with five pendulous petals that curve together, forming a globe surrounding a large green style shaped like an upside-down umbrella. From the point of view of a pollinator, this is not an easy drive-through for pollen and nectar; it takes some effort to enter and exit the floral labyrinth. The primary pollinators for northern pitcher plants are bumblebees (genus *Bombus*)—and not just any bumblebee, but the queen herself. In early spring, as queen bees emerge and begin searching for nest sites, they need constant and abundant feeding. The pitcher plant, with its ample supply of nectar, offers what the queen requires. In exchange, she has the size and strength to be an effective pollinator, visiting dozens of flowers in a day. Insect pollinators, though, are at risk for becoming prey. How does a carnivorous pitcher plant that depends on insect pollinators avoid trapping the very insects it needs to reproduce? One safety measure is spatial separation: Each flower hangs from a single stem that rises a good ten inches or more above the pitcher leaves. Another protective adaptation is timing. Many pitcher plants bloom in early spring (when their key pollinators are active) while their young, green leaves have not fully opened and the entrance to the pitcher remains closed.

Almost hidden in the moss was a miniature jewel box of a plant, the round-leaved sundew. A carnivorous species like the pitcher plant, it has its own strategy for capturing insects. Threadlike tentacles extend from its leaves, like tiny hands with outstretched fingers. These fingers are sticky with drops of viscous fluid that sparkle in the dim light—thus the name sundew. The shiny droplets produced by the plant attract small insects, then trap them with an adhesive grip. As the insect struggles to free itself, the movement triggers a physiological reaction in the sundew, causing its leaf to fold closed, trapping the insect inside. The plant produces chemicals that act as digestive enzymes, absorbing nutrients from the insect—a valuable survival skill in a nutrient-poor environment.

Charles Darwin was fascinated with insect-trapping plants, sundews in particular, for their example of how plants adapt to environmental conditions. He understood that insects and animals provide a dietary supplement to carnivorous plants but still are not its main source of nourishment. Photosynthesis is the process that drives growth and reproduction; sunlight, water, and carbon dioxide are the necessary ingredients for photosynthesis, but plants also need oxygen for cellular respiration. Where oxygen is limited, as it is in the deeper layers of the peatland, plants must adapt to this deprivation as well.

My gaze drifted upward from the flowered jewels at my feet to the spiky crowns of conifers around me. In an upland forest these trees might be nearly twice as tall, but here in the bog the scarcity of resources renders them short and slender in stature. Some of the dark tree trunks teeter at an angle, unable to remain upright. One of these notable trees is the tamarack, also known as eastern larch or by the Algonquin term, *hackmatack*. Even in its prime, a tamarack can be spindly and frail-looking, as if it could easily snap in a stiff wind—which they often do. There is a graceful beauty to these trees, though, their scaly branches lined with clusters of feathery needles and small round cones that resemble delicately carved wood roses. Tamaracks do well in peatlands, adapted to wetland life by producing shallow lateral roots that spread wide rather than deep. They arise in the hummocks of the bog, where beds of *Sphagnum* moss create the ideal conditions for germination of tamarack seeds. Over time, these hummock islands accrue enough elevated territory to support small copses of trees and shrubs. One thing tamaracks need is full sun; these trees will dwindle if black spruce or other more shade-tolerant tree species become established. The tamarack is a deciduous conifer; it comes to life in spring, when seemingly dead snags burst out with clusters of soft, jade green needles and the adornment of female cones bright as ripe raspberries. In fall, tamaracks are easily noticed by the honey-yellow needles that seem to glow in autumn light before they drop from the trees, adding to the layer of organic matter that becomes peat. Shedding needles allows the tamarack to survive intensely cold winters. It is a tree of the true north, widely found across the boreal forests of Canada up to the Arctic Circle.

Like peatlands to the north, the history of this habitat is linked to a glacial past of more than ten thousand years. The creation and history of the peatland is entwined with the climatic and ecological shifts that occurred at the end of the Pleistocene. Some fifteen thousand years ago ice covered much of the continent; beyond the glaciers' reach the landscape reflected a colder climate, covered by vast stretches of tundra and boreal forest resembling much of Canada's present-day muskeg. As the climate warmed, pioneer plants moved in, replacing willows and grasses with spruce woods. Where a particular mix of rainfall, temperature, and topography converges, plant species that now inhabit the boreal north are still found here, in the mountains of Pennsylvania, some at the southernmost extent of their geographic ranges. What I found at Tannersville Cranberry Bog Preserve was a small slice of peatland shaped by glacial history. Standing tentatively on the uneven boardwalk, I was not far from what had been the edge of the ice.

Now, in place of ice and snow, I was surrounded by a blanket of *Sphagnum* moss intersected with small cranberry, a dwarf creeping shrub that weaves its delicate branches across the surface. Whatever surface appearances of a thick, leafy carpet of moss may suggest, this place is essentially a water world. To take one step off the boardwalk—which protects the bog as much as the visiting bog-walker—is to take a slow plunge into another dimension that is neither liquid nor solid.

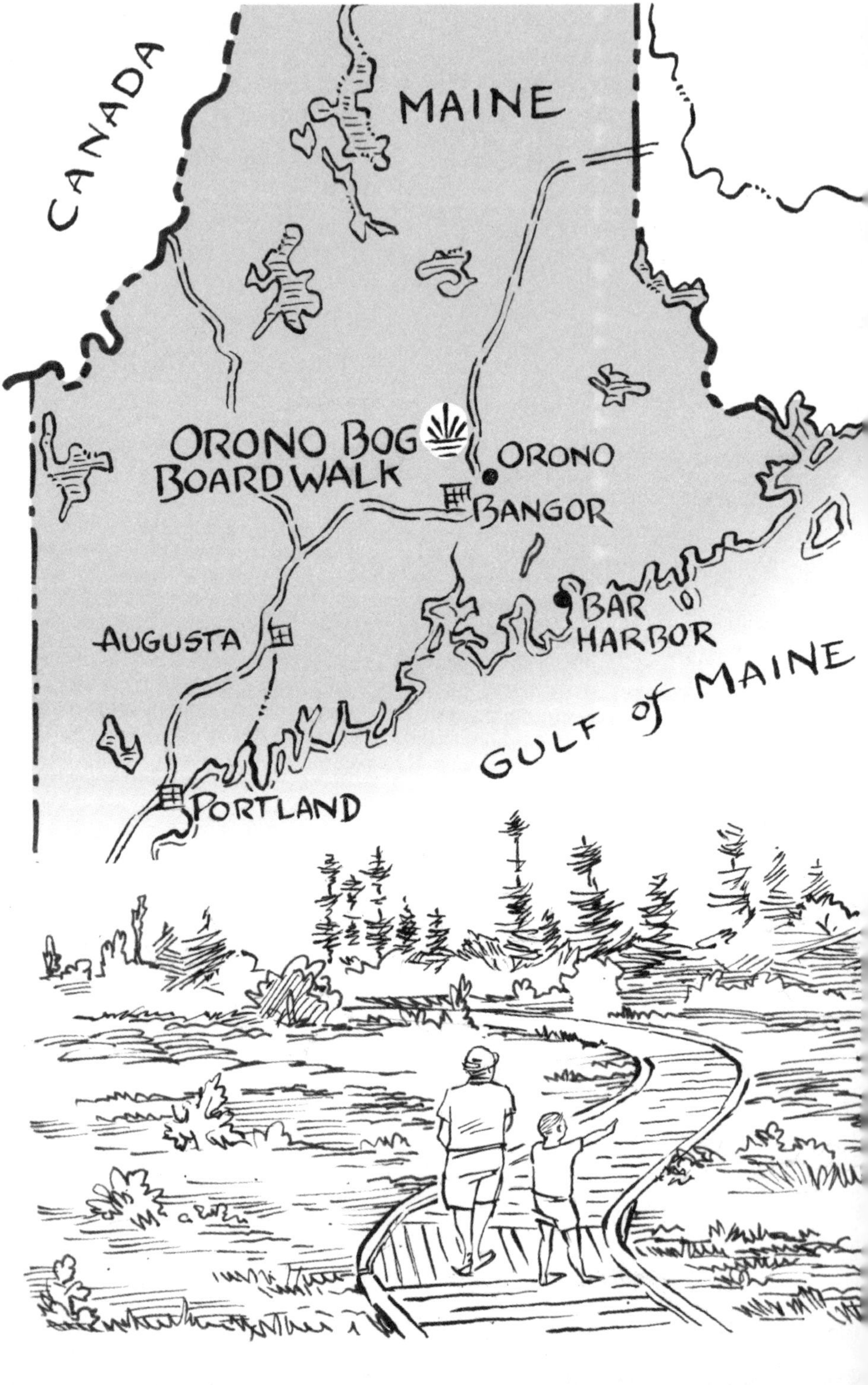
CANADA
MAINE
ORONO BOG
BOARDWALK
ORONO
BANGOR
AUGUSTA
BAR
HARBOR
GULF of MAINE
PORTLAND

FIVE

Bog Builders

Orono Bog, Maine

If I were to write a manual for how to build a peatland, it might start like this poem by Emily Dickinson:

> To make a prairie it takes a clover and one bee,
> One clover, and a bee.
> And revery.
> The revery alone will do,
> If bees are few.

But instead of a clover and a bee, I could begin with moss and sedge. Across much of North America, these are the plants that colonized the barren landscapes of gravel and glacial meltwater as the ice sheets of the Pleistocene retreated northward at the close of the last Ice Age. These pioneers laid down a welcome mat of organic matter for other plants to follow in a succession of ecological communities, from open lake to sedge fen, then to wooded fen, and eventually to moss-dominated bog. The diversity of life in a peatland is more complex and nuanced, but to understand these key actors is a light into the depths of the peat itself.

Of the more than ten thousand species of moss in the world, those of the genus *Sphagnum* hold a special place as a builder of peat. There are some 150 or more species of *Sphagnum,* most widely distributed in the Northern Hemisphere and closely associated with peatlands. *Sphagnum* species, more familiarly called peat mosses, are not simply acclimated to their environment; they actually help to create the conditions to which they are ideally suited. *Sphagnum* mosses thrive where many other plants cannot, a fact that ensures their survival and even dominance in peatland ecosystems. They cultivate their preferred habitat in two ways, by keeping it wet and acidic.

Sphagnum mosses are well designed to absorb and hold water, both in their body structure and at the cellular level. An individual *Sphagnum* plant has a large, shaggy head with thick clusters of leafy branches. Some of these branches spread outward, while others hang in slender green pendants. Stems and branches are thickly covered in tiny leaves, set close together and overlapping in a spiral pattern. Every nook and cranny of the *Sphagnum* anatomy helps the individual plant to hold water. When many thousands of *Sphagnum* plants grow together in a lush thicket of moss, their ability to hold moisture is magnified many times over. This capacity to retain water is even more impressive at a microscopic scale. It is a simple but elegant design: *Sphagnum* leaves are composed of two kinds of cells, living and dead. The living cells contain chlorophyll and thus are the engines of photosynthesis that fuels plant growth. The dead cells are, essentially, water tanks with porous, flexible walls that allow them to enlarge as they fill with water through capillary action, much the way a sponge expands as it soaks up liquid. The dead cells greatly outnumber the living cells, thus giving the plant its gift for absorption. Each leaf consists of a narrow band of living cells adjacent to a long chain of lifeless but essential water-storage units. Each *Sphagnum* plant grows upward from the crown of the plant as the lower submerged part of the plant dies, while the long stem of *Sphagnum* remains connected, deep into the watery peat.

Sphagnum holds another key to building a peatland by changing the pH of its environment. These mosses influence the chemistry of their surroundings by increasing acidity through the exchange of mineral ions. By taking up calcium, sodium, and other minerals and releasing hydrogen, *Sphagnum* transforms its wetland surroundings into an acidic habitat that is intolerable to many other plants. This chemistry trick works best under the conditions in an ombrotrophic bog—the kind of peatland that receives moisture only from the atmosphere. In minerotrophic fens, where water may also come from groundwater or surface runoff from uplands, the increased availability of nutrients allows for a wider variety of plant species; *Sphagnum* mosses are often present in fens, with different species found along a pH gradient—some preferring more or less acidic conditions.

While *Sphagnum* occupies the spotlight as a bog builder, at least in northern latitudes, mosses are not the only plants that are foundational to peatlands. The large family of sedges (Cyperaceae) includes more than a hundred species that flourish in fens and bogs. Sedges are often the structural engineers that help build the stage for peat formation. Growing along the exposed edges of shallow water, they weave a mat of roots and rhizomes on which *Sphagnum* and other peatland plants can gain a foothold in the wetland. The underground part of a sedge plant forms the bulk of its total biomass; the plants produce more living material below the surface than above. In sedge-dominated fens, it is the accumulated tangle of roots that contribute to the growing body of peat more than the leaves that die and decay into the litter at the surface.

Sedges can grow in dense swaths, dominated by one or several species, giving the appearance of a wet meadow. Some sedges form tussocks, contributing to a hummock-and-hollow topography that provides a variety of ecological niches for peatland plants. Adapted to wet habitats, sedges still have their preferences for varying conditions—acidity, nutrients, shade—with some thriving in bogs, and many others found in fens. Unlike mosses, sedges are flowering plants; they resemble grasses, but "sedges have edges," with long narrow leaves on solid, triangular stems. The diversity of species is displayed in a wild array of flowers that form spiky seed clusters, some that hang like ornaments from arching stems, others that burst like fireworks. Some of the most easily recognizable are the cotton sedges of the genus *Eriophorum* (also called cotton grasses, though they are not in the grass family).

Mosses and sedges are not the only heroes of this story. Shrubs in the heath family (Ericaceae) are fundamental to the structure and ecology of peatlands. Blueberries, cranberries, laurels, and leatherleaf are familiar companions to the mossy understory and the neighboring spruce and tamarack. There are animals, too—birds and mammals, insects and spiders—species that inhabit the understory of the shrub heath, tunnel into the matrix of the sedge mats, or pause in the wooded hummocks on their migratory travels. All are integral parts of a peatland, tolerating its extremes and contributing to the archive of its history, layer by layer.

One of the largest wetland systems in Maine, Caribou Bog, has glacial origins shaped by both ocean and ice. In the late Pleistocene era, some twenty thousand years ago, the Laurentide Ice Sheet extended out to what is now known as Georges Bank, a vast stretch of sea floor lying between present-day Cape Cod and Nova Scotia. As the climate warmed the ice sheet began to retreat northward, deeply scouring the bedrock beneath it along the way. The seas moved inland, filling the lowlands as the glacial ice withdrew. The ocean waters reached their farthest extent landward about twelve thousand years ago, and while they covered the continental surface, layers of marine sediments accumulated. Runoff from the melting ice also contributed a slurry of finely ground rock to the layers of silt. Millennia of bearing the weight of ice had depressed the land surface beneath. Over time, the land began to rebound, slowly rising in elevation after being relieved of its glacial burden. As the land rose, the sea retreated, leaving behind the marine silts that coated the surface, forming an impervious layer like a glaze on a pottery bowl. The shaping of the land surface by the ice sheets, combined with the deposit of marine and glacial sediments, prepared the scene for wetland plant communities to take hold.

After the ice and ocean retreated, a large lowland basin was filled by freshwater, prevented from draining by the impermeable marine layers. About eight thousand years ago, sedge fens developed between pockets of open water. These fen islands offered a foothold for larger woody shrubs and trees, and eventually a wooded fen habitat dominated by tamarack trees emerged. As the plants grew and died, building ever greater stores of peat, the conditions were ideal for mosses to become established. The mosses further altered their habitat as acidity increased and nutrients decreased; by around five thousand years ago, *Sphagnum* dominated the peatlands we see today. One of the best places to experience this landscape is in the southern reach of Caribou Bog, known by the name of the nearby community: Orono Bog.

The Orono Bog boardwalk, on the outskirts of Bangor, Maine, is like a large picture book: rich with illustrations, thoughtfully translated, inviting to many kinds of readers. It opens the often-hidden world of peatlands and makes it visible—to the casual walker, the parent pushing a stroller, the student on a field trip. Like the boardwalk at Tannersville Cranberry Bog, it allows visitors to create an imprint in their imaginations without leaving footprints in the peat. The Orono Bog boardwalk covers a loop of just under a mile, making a transect from the outer edge of the upland forest to the center of the domed bog. Following the interpretive stations along the way, the walker is persuaded to pause and admire the qualities of each of the plant communities. The intention to educate is driven by the University of Maine, which owns the 616-acre tract that encompasses Orono Bog, in partnership with the City of Bangor and the Orono Land Trust. Since the boardwalk opened to the public in 2003, hundreds of students, dozens of scientists, and thousands of visitors have trod across the planks that lead into the bog. The care and stewardship of Orono Bog makes it one of the most accessible peatland sites to explore as a self-guided bog-walker. But you will not be alone. The popularity of the site in good weather ensures the company of other bog enthusiasts and the merely curious.

I arrived on a Monday morning, with late September sun slanting through the trees, warming the air enough to catch a whiff of balsam fir and the dusty scent of dry leaves. A short path led me to a trail junction: to the left, a network of trails through Bangor City Forest; to the right, the entrance to Orono Bog. On entering the boardwalk, I passed through a broad-leaved forest of red maple and black ash with leafy thickets of speckled alder. In the dappled light of deciduous trees, the air felt warm and familiar—eastern woods in autumn. I passed over a moat of sorts called a *lagg*, the shallow margin between the peatland and upland. Water draining off the higher ground carries nutrients and minerals, enriching the plant life in this transition zone. A black-capped chickadee flitted by at eye level, darting between the leafy shrubs and an opening of light created by a fallen tree. Chipping sparrows and red-breasted nuthatches chattered and buzzed, moving between the forest canopy and the open shrubland ahead of me.

Following a slight rise in elevation brought me to an island of a few isolated clusters of small trees punctuating the shrub heath, with dwarfed black spruces no taller than me and spindly tamaracks crouched low to the ground. The gentle slope was revealed by the presence of these conifers: The trees tolerate acidic soils but still need enough height above the water table to support a network of roots in the shallow layer of aerated soil. The ascent was barely noticeable except for the changes in plant life, but it signified the shape and history of the bog: a broad, convex dome created by the steady accumulation of peat over thousands of years. A cluster of black spruces grew in a ring, like a crown on top of the hummock. The lower branches grazed the ground; in places, they nestled below the thick moss layer. If I were to dig down into the *Sphagnum,* I would find older tree branches that had been blanketed by the moss and, once covered, sent up shoots to become new trees, genetically identical to the parent tree. This process, called layering, keeps producing young clones as the *Sphagnum* keeps pace, deepening the peat in which the trees are rooted.

As I continued to the north, the boardwalk led out into an open expanse of shrub heath, so named because many of the woody plants found here are in the heath family, Ericaceae. This also explains the local names for many peatlands in Maine: Big Heath, Great Heath, Saco Heath, and Jonesport Heath, among others. All around me I could see a profusion of Ericaceae family members, woven together in a thigh-high labyrinth of woody branches and thick leaves. True to its name, leatherleaf covers large swaths of the open peat bog with its tough, olive-green foliage.

Thickets of the sun-loving leatherleaf are so dense that they shade out seedlings of trees or tall shrubs that might compete. I recognized Labrador tea by its spicy fragrance which, the story goes, Thoreau once described as a blend of turpentine and strawberries. The delicate and diminutive bog rosemary has in common with other heath shrubs narrow leaves that roll inward from the edge, clad with a furry underside. The features once thought to be adaptations to reduce water loss seem out of place in a saturated peatland; alternative hypotheses suggest that thick, furry leaves are an advantage in a nutrient-poor environment or help the plant tolerate temperature extremes. Some botanists point to these characteristics as common to many heath family species, whether found in peatlands or other habitats. Many heath species adapt to low-nutrient conditions by forming root–fungus partnerships, known as *mycorrhizal associations*—a more common strategy of peatland shrubs and some trees. The mycorrhizae, which are tiny filaments produced by fungi, connect with the fine roots of the host plant, providing nitrogen and phosphorus to the plant in exchange for simple sugars, the products of the vascular plant's photosynthesis.

As I approached the farthest point on the boardwalk loop, the open bog transformed again into a sort of magic carpet with lush shades of wine-red, yellow-green, and smoky brown blended into a textured pool of color. This was the bull's-eye shown on the map at the trailhead, a centerpiece of the bog modestly called a moss lawn. Here was a kingdom ruled by *Sphagnum* mosses, where the water hovers close to the surface, rising in wet periods of rain or snow melt. Water comes from the sky and is held closely by the peat below.

In her book *Gathering Moss: A Natural and Cultural History of Mosses*, botanist Robin Wall Kimmerer writes, "mosses are the amphibians of the plant world." Like frogs and salamanders, mosses are dependent on both water and air. Moisture must be directly accessible to allow mosses to photosynthesize, grow, and reproduce. This dependence on water is, in part, due to their evolutionary history. Mosses are descendants of green algae, some of the first land plants that evolved nearly five hundred million years ago. In their migration onto land, they adapted to a wide range of microhabitats. For all the diversity of mosses, one thing they have in common is their diminutive size. Mosses are small for a reason. In their transition to life on land they developed leaves, stems, and cellular structures suited to wet environments. But they did not develop the ability to produce true roots or vascular tissue—two fundamental components of most other classes of plants. Ferns, conifers, and flowering plants all possess xylem and phloem, specialized tissues that create a cellular-level delivery system for conducting water and nutrients throughout the plant. From the tip of a taproot to the crown of a tree, vascular plants are capable of moving food and water great distances. Not so for the mosses. Without roots or vascular tissue, mosses cannot conduct water or nutrients from the soil into their living tissue. Instead, they rely on capillary action, wicking up and moving water through the physical attributes of water molecules. This mechanism requires no energy on the part of the moss, but it does have its limits. Capillary action will move water only so far, and thus mosses keep close to the ground.

Varieties of moss can be a signature to the conditions of bog and fen; looking at the uneven, rumpled surface of a peatland offers clues to the habitat preferences of different species. In the open peatland with plenty of sun, feathery bogmoss fills the deepest hollows close to the water table with long, sweeping branches of pale green. One of the most aquatic of the *Sphagnum* mosses, when removed from the water it slumps into a limp tangle. On floating peat mats, Magellan's peatmoss covers large swaths in burgundy red. Nestled nearby is its plump, golden-brown cousin, fat bog moss, or papillose *Sphagnum*. The *Sphagnum* species found on the hummocks keep their heads above water; to help reduce water loss they grow closely packed, their stems and branches more erect than the mosses in the wet hollows. Red peatmoss, for example, is a rosy-hued species that favors the midelevations of hummocks, while rusty bogmoss, a dense, brown moss, grows on the driest crown of the hummock.

This assembly of species, adapted to the extremes of wetness, acidity, and a lack of oxygen and nutrients, are remarkable in their perseverance. Microhabitats in this community are like neighborhoods: the moss-filled bowls, the sheltered tamarack islands, the impenetrable maze of the shrub heath. Each species has its own place in the community, but still it needs to survive changing conditions over time, day and night, season to season.

I stood at the far end of the boardwalk, looking out at the pillow-topped spread of moss lawn, embroidered with strands of cranberry and dotted with tawny cottonsedge. The warm September day was one of several consecutive days without rain, and long after the melting snows of spring. It was dry season in the bog, and the tops of the hummocks showed a slight crispiness, colors fading in the full sun. Here the landscape took on a northerly aspect, a kind of stoic elegance of plants adapted to endure long, frigid winters. In the warmth of midmorning, I could feel the collective energy of photosynthesis taking place around me, the forest making the most of these last warm days to capture the light fueling its growth and ensuring its survival in the cold months to come. For five thousand years, Orono Bog has endured wet years, dry seasons, fire, sun, and storm. The peat moss deepens, black spruces arise from the buried branches of ancestor trees, the heath hums with summer insects and grows silent under snow.

BOG CRANBERRY

SIX

Outflow

Pine Barrens, New Jersey

Without water, what is a wetland? A water world thirsting for its true self. Water from the heavens, from inflowing streams, spreading overland after a rainstorm, or rising up to the surface from aquifers hidden below. On earth, water is both abundant and finite. Most of the world's water exists as saltwater in its vast oceans. Only 2.5 percent of the planet's water is freshwater, and two-thirds of that freshwater is bound up in glaciers and polar ice caps. A tiny fraction of freshwater is found at the surface or just below it—in lakes, marshes, and in soil moisture. Freshwater is what all creatures are drawn to, for sustenance and survival. I feel this pull, like a dowsing rod, even where the body of water is concealed in the depths of peat beneath a blanket of moss.

When a peatland loses its water, physical, chemical, and biological changes alter the ecosystem. There is a visible loss of elevation; the peat shrinks as it dries and becomes consolidated. When a peatland is drained, it can subside by an inch per year, or six to eight feet over a century. The chemistry of peatland soils changes too, as air penetrates the spaces once filled with water. Exposed to the elements, the upper layer of peat breaks down at an accelerated rate, and the carbon once locked inside is released to the atmosphere as carbon dioxide.

The residents of the neighborhood change as well. Microbes and invertebrates that could not survive in the waterlogged condition of undisturbed peat now find a more hospitable environment. Decay and decomposition take off, digesting the stored carbon in the peat. Vegetation shifts as the newly aerated soils allow deeper roots established by a wide range of plant species. Drained peatlands may quickly become forested, as if the trees waited on the margins for the high tide to ebb, allowing them a footing in the rich organic soils.

In my explorations, I found many peatlands that suffered from these losses. Many more were gone forever, no longer discernible as wetlands. The drainage of peatlands results from many different activities—some intentional, some not. Ditching and draining peatlands has a long history in Europe. Immigrants to the New World brought with them the traditions, tools, and technology for draining wetlands to reclaim land for agriculture and forestry. For more than three hundred years, wetlands of all kinds have been drained, degraded, and converted to other uses.

All this destruction stems from the combined energy of two forces: fear of wild places, and desire for economic gain. In the seventeenth and eighteenth centuries, swamps, marshes, and bogs were viewed by white settlers as wastelands: inconvenient and unpleasant at best, unhealthy and dangerous at worst. At the same time, the fever for accumulating land was growing rapidly, and acquiring and keeping title to land depended on its "improvement"—to turn a profit and recover the purchase debt, or sometimes as a condition of a land grant. Land speculators were considered visionaries who saw ways to reshape wild wetlands into prosperous farms and towns. The nineteenth and twentieth centuries saw the rise of new technologies that made it faster and easier to rearrange landscapes on a broad scale. Steam power replaced much of the need for hard labor by hand, while the production and use of drainage tiles became widespread.

Throughout the early twentieth century, US government policies generally aided and abetted the draining of wetlands. Federal agricultural agencies provided technical assistance and funding to farmers to promote drainage projects; other government programs subsidized wetland conversion as part of flood control and public works projects. Between the mid-1950s and mid-1970s, nearly 90 percent of wetland losses were the result of agricultural practices. Then public perception began to shift in the 1970s, driven by outdoor sportsmen and wetland scientists, bird-watchers and Boy Scouts. Gradually, elected officials recognized that wetlands were valuable *as wetlands*—providing wildlife with habitat, clean water, and flood protection. The emerging science of ecology and the growing conservation movement built a powerful headwind against the forces that had driven wetland destruction for centuries. Marshes and bogs were increasingly viewed as part of America's great wilderness legacy, places to protect and restore. In 1985, the federal Farm Bill added a new component, the "Highly Erodible Land Conservation and Wetland Conservation Compliance" provisions, known as the Swampbuster Act, that removed incentives for the conversion of wetlands to croplands. Farming on wetland soils would make a landowner ineligible for federal crop subsidies. Along with the federal Clean Water Act, conversion of wetlands now required mitigation through the enhancement or restoration of existing wetland habitat to offset the losses from any alteration or loss of wetlands.

The loss of peatlands, marshes, and swamps occurs both swiftly and slowly. Reshaping the earth, whether digging by hand or with modern machinery, creates dramatic changes in living systems. The persistent drive to ditch and drain wet places has long-term consequences, a kind of death by a thousand cuts. Happily, a reversal is underway, but the process of restoration is slow by comparison. Federal and state policies have changed over the past forty years, yet trying to undo the damage will take another half century, or more. Species that have been displaced don't always magically reappear; the flow of water doesn't necessarily follow the same pathways. Changes in these ecosystems will continue over decades and longer, with or without the force of the human hand.

On the southern outer coastal plain of New Jersey lies a wilderness, a green footprint amidst one of the most densely urbanized states on the East Coast. Originally more than one million acres of land, situated between Philadelphia and New York City, much of it endures as forest. Dominated by pitch pine and oaks, the Pine Barrens is like an isolated country, persistent in its identity of place as the rest of the world around it changes. Though sparsely populated, the Pine Barrens has a long human history, like a tangled undergrowth among the seemingly endless pine forests. Logging, charcoal, iron, glass—industries have come and gone, leaving changes on the land. In the sandy soils of the region, agriculture is mostly limited to cultivation of native blueberries and cranberries. The name "Barrens" is misleading, though. One of its remarkable features, known to Indigenous peoples, white settlers, and development boosters of the twentieth century, is the abundance of water. Pure water, originating as rainfall, stored as groundwater, and moving slowly through the network of waterways above- and belowground.

Underlying the sandy surface or exposed on the surface of wetlands, the Kirkwood-Cohansey Aquifer typically sits just a few feet below the dry areas of the Pine Barrens, supplying most of the base flow to streams, rivers, and wetlands. An aquifer is both a geologic and hydrologic feature: a layer of sand or rock porous and permeable enough to hold water in the tiny spaces between the grains. These groundwater systems are extremely variable, both in time and space. Water flows belowground at rates much slower than surface flows. A velocity of one foot per day is a fairly high rate for groundwater, compared to stream flows that are measured in feet per second. In the Pine Barrens, surface water is relatively slow moving because of the low-lying topography of the coastal plain. Water flows, above and below the surface, follow the subtle dip of lowlands and the general tilt of the plain toward the east and south, eventually reaching the Atlantic Ocean and Delaware Bay.

Within the sprawling Pine Barrens, a patchwork of large and small tracts of land have been protected by state and private conservation efforts. At nearly ten thousand acres, the Franklin Parker Preserve is part of a larger complex of public conservation lands that protects about a quarter-million acres of the Pine Barrens. I found my way to Franklin Parker Preserve one early October, when the Pine Barrens glowed with russet, bronze, and plum colors of autumn. I had arranged to meet with Emile DeVito and Russell Juelg, both scientists with the New Jersey Conservation Foundation, which owns and manages the preserve. Joined by a couple of student researchers, our small group drove in a caravan along a network of dike roads that crisscross the wetland complex, stopping first at a wooden viewing platform. In this broad horizon of the coastal plain, elevation is perspective. From a bird's-eye view, a broad mantle of hummocky wetlands extended to a distant perimeter of pine-oak forest.

Emile had offered to guide me through an afternoon's exploration of the preserve and its centerpiece: more than a thousand acres of a former cranberry farm, now converted to wetlands through a seven-year restoration effort completed in late 2011. The massive project required re-engineering a highly controlled system. Dikes were breached to allow water flows to rise and fall with the natural cycle of rainfall; drainage canals were plugged and spillways modified. Earth-moving equipment was used to reshape the surface, turning giant scoopfuls of soil and sand to create high and low spots where water could pool during wet periods or provide islands where vegetation could gain a foothold above the water table.

Before remaking the landscape, scientists examined test samples of the deep soil to ensure that a viable seed bank still existed; once these deeper soils were unearthed and brought to the surface, the wetland ecosystem could regenerate native vegetation with the diversity and richness of the natural landscape that predated the cranberry farm. Now, a decade later, the restored wetlands are lush with plants and shrubs like leatherleaf and highbush blueberry. Restoration of water flows, or “rewetting the wetlands,” reclaims habitat for plants and animals. It also serves another valuable function: restarting the development of peat. The rapid decomposition that occurred when the cranberry fields were drained is slowed dramatically when natural hydrological cycles are restored. The saturated soils hold onto the carbon taken up by the now diverse plant community. As the plants grow, photosynthesize, and store carbon in their leaves, stems, and roots, that plant material accumulates in the wet earth and turns gradually into peat.

A natural peat bog provides the wet and acidic conditions in which native cranberries thrive. Since cranberries were first cultivated in the 1800s, farmers have sought to modify these conditions to increase production and improve efficiency in growing and harvesting a valuable crop. Modern cranberry farming makes radical changes in soil, topography, and hydrology—a major alteration of a wetland ecosystem. The creation of a modern commercial cranberry bog requires removal of the vegetation and upper layer of topsoil, followed by careful layering of silt, sand, topsoil, and more sand. The engineering required is impressive. Each layer is leveled flat, like a rice paddy, to ensure consistent water levels throughout the field. Drainage and irrigation systems are installed throughout a network of perimeter dikes, constructed to at least a foot above the surface of the bog, that allow access for managing fields and harvesting the crop. These embankments also separate growing bogs from adjacent reservoirs where water is held until fall, when the stored water is shunted through canals and water control structures to flow into the cranberry bog.

The dike and drainage systems ensure control of water levels throughout the year. A grid of ditches etched into the fields drains excess water away in the spring, when the cranberry shrubs' tender buds begin to grow as temperatures warm. Throughout the growing season, cranberries need a steady supply of water, either from rainfall or irrigation. Some farmers also use spray irrigation to water the vines in case of a late frost or a spell of hot, windy weather. Growing cranberries demands a significant amount of water throughout the annual cycle, using seven to ten feet of water per acre over the year for growing, harvesting, and winter protection, though some of that water is reused by channeling it from one field to the next over the harvest period. In fall, at harvest time, fields are flooded to a depth of a foot of water. This flooding is an essential part of the modern harvest technique: Ripe cranberries are buoyant and rise to the surface of the newly flooded fields. Modern farmers use water-reel harvesting equipment called "water beaters" that loosen the berries from the vines so they float on the water surface, where they can be corralled with a boom system into a suction pump or conveyor that delivers the berries to a waiting truck. After the harvest, the bogs are kept flooded throughout the winter months to protect the vines from frost.

Cranberry harvests were once less mechanized, requiring many hours of picking by hand. The harvesting tool of the nineteenth and early twentieth century was a wooden cranberry scoop, a sort of coarse comb attached to a small box, used to gently strip the ripe berries from the vines. Dry harvesting is still done in small farm operations, mainly for the higher-value crop of berries sold fresh.

Cranberries are members of the heath family, Ericaceae, that thrive in nutrient-poor, acidic soils. The genus, *Vaccinium,* is shared by blueberries and cranberries, both found in and around peatlands in North America. Though in cultivation the plants are often referred to as vines, cranberries are more accurately described as creeping shrubs, with evergreen leaves and small whitish-pink flowers. The large cranberry is the native species from which cultivated varieties have been developed since the early nineteenth century, when ship captain Henry Hall retired to his farm in Cape Cod, Massachusetts, and began tinkering with growing berries. He observed that the plants grew best in sandy pockets that were on the dry side in summer and wet in winter. The vines sent up shoots through the windblown sand and produced large, plump berries. Captain Hall experimented with transplanting vines and tailoring the growing conditions to improve the quality and yield of his crop. His neighbors took notice, and more growers began planting sandy acres in cranberry vines and tinkering with different root stocks to select for the largest, most flavorful berries. Eventually, word spread to New Jersey, where residents of the Pine Barrens recognized that their sandy soils offered the same growing conditions for a wild berry that now had an emerging commercial market.

Long before cultivation and development of hybrid varieties, however, Indigenous people gathered cranberries, using them as food and medicine. The Lenni Lenape of New Jersey, like other native people from Canada to the Carolinas, ate cranberries both fresh and dried and often mixed into prepared foods like pemmican, using a combination of cranberries, dried venison, and fat. *Pakihm,* the Lenape word for cranberry, was also valued for its healing properties as a poultice for wounds. One *sachem,* or chief, of the Lenni Lenape was called *Pakimintzen,* meaning "cranberry eater," as an acknowledgment of the cranberry as a symbol of peace and goodwill.

As the afternoon sun began its slow descent to the west, my guides and I zigzagged our way through the preserve toward the overlapping margins between wetland and forest, where Emile's students, Jordan and Alex, used radio telemetry to search for the den of a northern pine snake. Emile navigated the maze of sand roads to a specific location where radio signals were recently picked up. Alex held an antenna with one hand and adjusted the receiver with the other, listening for faint pings to point him in the right direction. Monitoring the populations and movements of pine snakes is one of many scientific research efforts ongoing at the preserve. Emile has been coordinating projects like this one for more than thirty years; the students listened intently to his instruction as we walked briskly along a sandy path. I listened too, as Emile unspooled story after story about the nature of the pinelands, the history of the preserve, the habits of pine snakes. He described the Pine Barrens as being akin to a prairie, only with a lot more rain and thus supporting trees instead of grass. The pitch pine that dominates this ecosystem is like the big bluestem, forming a dense, uniform vegetation that is resilient and adapted to fire.

Another signature tree species found in the Pine Barrens, though less abundant, is the Atlantic white cedar. Not a true cedar but a member of the cypress family, the white cedar is found within a fifty-mile swath of the Atlantic coast from Maine to Florida, and in parts of the Gulf Coast. In the seemingly flat landscape of the Pine Barrens, the cedar is strictly a lowland species, while the pitch pine is mainly an upland tree but also found in wetlands. The Atlantic white cedar prefers the low-lying areas where the water table is close to the surface, keeping its feet wet and the air humid and cool.

Emile asked if I wanted to see a mature cedar forest, the source of the seed used to grow the Atlantic white cedar seedlings in the restoration project. I did indeed. We drove back across the preserve to the entrance gate near the village of Chatsworth; from there he led me to a spot just outside town. The road sliced through pine woods, where sun filtered through to the forest floor and wind lifted the needled branches in lazy swells. Through my open car window, the breathy hush of wind in pines floated through in a current of sound and fragrance. Then, as I rounded a sharp curve, I suddenly entered another atmosphere, cooler by several degrees and darker, as if time had jumped forward and dusk was rapidly approaching.

In the flat terrain of the Pine Barrens, a slight dip in topography often changes the growing conditions from pine-oak forest to cedar swamp. These are lowland forests, and where the water is close to the surface, the Atlantic white cedars form compact stands of straight trunks stretching up to seventy or eighty feet, packed so tightly together the branches with needles don't begin until high up in the canopy. At the base of the trees is a rumpled quilt of *Sphagnum* mosses, rounded and pockmarked with wet spots, littered with fallen branches. These lowland forests, Emile explained, follow the imprint of stream beds. He showed me aerial images: the pattern of darkest green tracing the outlines of stream drainage. The lowland elevation of waterways creates the conditions for cedars to grow. Exiting the car, we scrambled into a thicket of trees. Emile used a dead cedar branch to drive into the cover of soft moss, which sank easily to a depth of twenty inches or so. We could penetrate deeper with a longer probe, he noted, a suggestion that we were just scratching the surface. This was a small sample of the layers of peat and muck accumulating along these stream beds, under these cedars, fingering through the broader mosaic of the Pine Barrens ecosystem.

With apologies, Emile told me he had to get back to attend fieldwork at the preserve, but before leaving he sent me a text message with the latitude-longitude coordinates for an older forest of Atlantic white cedar at a place called Shinns Branch, one of the state's first designated Significant Natural Areas. I tapped the link on my phone and headed north. Turning off Highway 72, I entered Brendan T. Byrne State Forest and onto hard-packed sand roads through pitch pine forest. Driving on sand roads in the Pine Barrens is disorienting; the tracks are laid out in a seemingly endless grid pattern but never appear to align to compass points. There is no hint of whether you are heading north or south, into or out of the forest. My phone's directional system showed me I was nearing my destination, but all I saw were pines. The sun was bright again, and still autumn air wafted through the trees. My phone announced: "You have arrived." Wondering if I was somehow driving in circles, if I'd lost my way in a land without landmarks, I stopped for a moment. Ahead of me, the road seemed to lead into shadow. Pressing on, I slid into the imperceptible hollow of lowland and was wrapped again in the darkness of Atlantic white cedars.

The Atlantic white cedar swamp is not a place that can be fully perceived with the eyes. It is felt with other senses. It fills your lungs with something more than air—an elixir, a vapor laced with organic chemical compounds as complex and rich as wine, and just as intoxicating. The Japanese concept of *Shinrin-yoku,* or forest bathing, comes close to describing the ethereal experience of being in a deep and ancient forest. And yet, this forest is not ancient. Atlantic white cedars have been logged since the arrival of white settlers in the seventeenth century. Most forests have been cut over twice, or even three times, so that old-growth forests no longer exist. In the eighteenth century, many cedar swamps were clear-cut and converted to cranberry bogs. In the late 1800s, the persistent demand for Atlantic white cedar led to exhuming cedar logs buried deep in the swamps to be split into shingles and fence rails. Atlantic white cedar forests once covered 115,000 acres in New Jersey; recent estimates of existing acreage are fewer than 30,000 acres. The future of cedar forest in the Pine Barrens may be seeing a reversal of fortunes, however. The state's Department of Environmental Protection has launched an ambitious effort to restore between 10,000 and 20,000 acres of Atlantic white cedar forest over the next decade, with the assistance of nonprofit partners such as the New Jersey Conservation Foundation and the New Jersey Audubon Society.

Looking up into the crown of forest, the spires of tree trunks pointed like arrows toward the light. Trees do fall in the forest—the cedar is shallow-rooted and subject to windthrow—but some of these timbers were suspended when their fall was broken by neighboring trees, creating an etched silhouette of straight and angled lines. At eye level, the tree trunks are shaggy with deep, spiraled grooves. Although the foliage of the mature trees was far above my head, a broken limb lay nearby, and I knelt to examine the scaly needles arranged in flat sprays, still green and fragrant. My knees pressed into the lushness of *Sphagnum* mosses, a soft bed that conjures an image of Rip Van Winkle, and I could imagine being lured into a very long sleep in this magical forest. I noticed the dim light beginning to diminish further. It was late afternoon, and if I lingered much longer, I might find myself having to make my way home in the dark. I retraced my route on the sand roads and onto the highway. Out of the woods, for now.

PART III

carbon

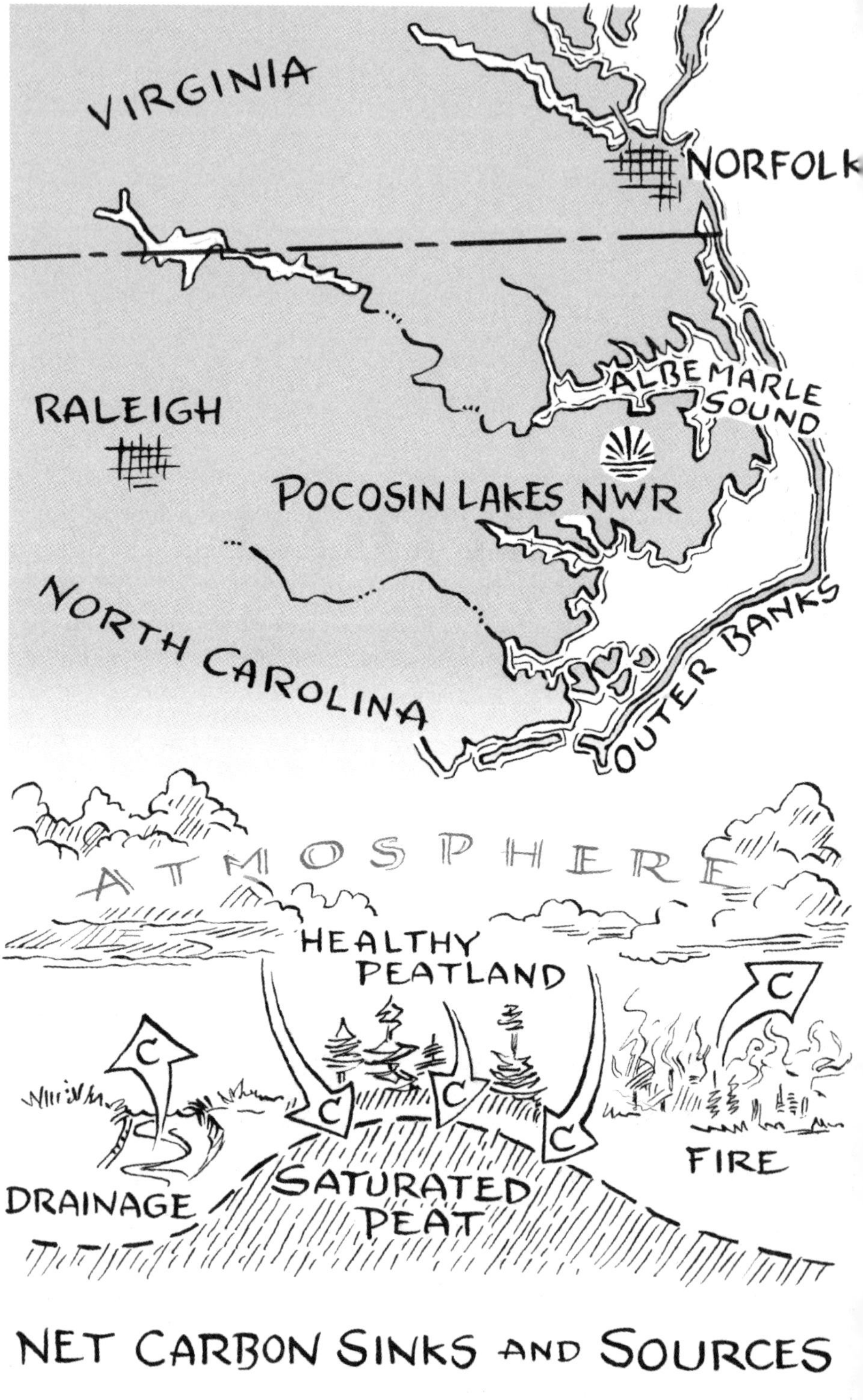

NET CARBON SINKS AND SOURCES

SEVEN

Sinks and Sources

Pocosin Lakes, North Carolina

Carbon is everywhere—in the air, the oceans, the earth, in the structure of every living thing. Carbon is a natural shape-shifter, seeking out attachments to other atoms to form a multitude of molecular structures that are essential components of organic life. Gregarious and restless, carbon moves as it reinvents itself, a perpetual voyager on the carbon cycle.

The many lives of a single atom of carbon over hundreds of millions of years is a story best told by Primo Levi, an Italian scientist and writer of the mid-twentieth century, in his collection of essays titled *The Periodic Table.* The final chapter begins with a carbon atom passing eons deep in the mineral crust of Earth, bound with oxygen and calcium in a piece of limestone. Eventually, the rock shelf containing this atom is exposed at the surface and broken into pieces by the hand of an axe-wielding man. The man feeds the rock into a lime kiln, where combustion separates the carbon calcite components and sends the atom into the atmosphere in a molecule of carbon dioxide. The carbon atom becomes a traveler, shifting between the atmosphere and the oceans, borne along on the wind and water. At last the atom is captured from the air by the process of photosynthesis as it is drawn into a tiny porthole, or stomata, on the leaf of a grapevine. The carbon binds with other atoms to form glucose and becomes part of the fruit that is picked, pressed, and fermented into wine. The wine is drunk by a farmer, and the carbon atom moves through the man's liver and muscles before being expelled in his breath. The atom dances along, partnering with other elements, becoming cellulose in the bark of a cedar tree, chitin in the eye of a moth. At last, the carbon is found in a glass of milk, swallowed by the writer, and flows into the blood and brain and hand of the man telling the tale of the atom's journey. Whether you read it in Levi's story or in a chemistry textbook, the carbon cycle represents how this essential element moves through the biosphere, hydrosphere, and atmosphere as carbon atoms are exchanged and recombined.

A cycle is both real and conceptual. Flows of energy, matter, or biological change move through processes that, from our time-limited human experience, seem endless. The simplicity of a circular form helps us visualize how one stage of being leads to another, and then another: A cycle helps us make sense of perpetuity. Carbon, in its myriad forms, moves through different pools or reservoirs and is stored for varying lengths of time. The cycle moves at different speeds. Carbon moves at its slowest pace in the geosphere, where it is sequestered in the earth's crust as carbonate minerals such as marine sediments composed of the shells of ancient sea creatures. In the atmosphere, carbon travels in gaseous forms of carbon dioxide, carbon monoxide, and methane. The world's oceans absorb carbon from the atmosphere through a dynamic exchange that occurs between the water surface and the air above. This interface, between air and oceans, drives short-term cycling between the two pools of carbon storage. In the terrestrial biosphere, carbon dioxide in the atmosphere is absorbed by plants through photosynthesis and used to produce sugars that bond to form chains of cellulose, which, in turn, creates the biomass stored in leaves, roots, and stems. Carbon is most abundant in the soil, which holds three times as much carbon as is found in living plants aboveground.

Carbon exists in all organisms, both living and dead. Branches break, leaves fall, roots wither. All the plant matter that falls to the ground begins a new cycle of decomposition. Bacteria, fungi, worms, slugs, all kinds of scavengers large and small do their part in the carbon cycle: It takes a village of organisms to break down plant tissue and return carbon and other elements back into the soil, water, and air. (Animals too release carbon when they die and decompose.) Some carbon is returned to the atmosphere as the plant respires (in a gas exchange through stomata in the leaves); some is released into the soil through plant roots. Some of the carbon embodied in plant tissue is transferred to animals eating plants.

This short-term cycling of carbon as it moves through photosynthesis, plant growth, death, and decomposition, and is released back to the atmosphere is described as carbon flux. The carbon flux between air, plants, and soil varies widely depending on environmental conditions and the chemistry of the organic matter involved. When more carbon is absorbed and stored in the plants and soils than is released to the atmosphere, the result is a carbon sink. Conversely, when more carbon is released into the air—either slowly, through decomposition, or quickly, through fire or rapid drainage—the result is a carbon source. Any given ecosystem can be a carbon sink or source, or even both at different times, switching from one to the other. Seasonal shifts occur between the growing season when plants are inhaling deeply, turning carbon into plant tissue, and the dormant season when photosynthesis shifts into low gear. Consider a young forest with rapidly growing trees that are drawing in enormous quantities of carbon dioxide and transforming that carbon, along with water and energy from sunlight, into leaves and wood. A healthy forest like this would likely be a sizable carbon sink. But if conditions change—say, if the trees are stressed by drought or an insect infestation—then the forest might suffer through slower growth and a depressed ability to photosynthesize. If the environmental conditions persist or worsen, trees will begin to die. The accelerating process of decomposition will shift some of the carbon stored in their leaves and branches back into carbon dioxide, turning the forest from a carbon sink into a carbon source.

Peatlands are natural carbon sinks. Peat develops where the amount of organic matter produced by plants exceeds the amount of organic matter that is broken down in decomposition, resulting in more carbon stored than released. The process of breaking down the accumulation of plant material is slowed by the watery nature of peat and lack of oxygen. Left undisturbed, the carbon stored in the depths of a peatland is locked away for millennia. Over the past ten thousand years or so, most peatlands have quietly kept stock of their accumulated carbon atoms. But shocks to the system—either abrupt disturbances or gradual but accelerating shifts in conditions—can trigger a change in carbon flux, from sink to source. Fire is one of the most dramatic shifts, altering peatlands from carbon sink to carbon source in days, even hours, as centuries of accumulated organic carbon are transformed into carbon dioxide. In a plume of smoke, millions of atoms are sent skyward in their endless journey through the carbon cycle.

A small chunk of dried peat is glowing in a dish on the table, sending up a thin curl of smoke. It fills the kitchen with a sweet, earthy fragrance, reminiscent of a campfire in drizzling rain. This fragment of organic matter is the embodied fuel of many plants, living and breathing over many years. The plants absorbed carbon dioxide from the air and used the carbon to build plant tissues; then as the plants died, leaves fell and branches were buried under the surface of moss or sedge. Water submerged the remains, and time compressed the layers of dark, rich material into a buried treasure of stored carbon. This bit of peat burning like incense in my kitchen was lifted from the earth, dried, and formed into small bricks for the purpose of creating a combustible fuel. But peat will burn even when it is still in the ground.

Wildfires can spark in living peatlands during periods of drought, or when peat soils are dried by exposure to air from ditching, draining, road building, or other disturbances. Anything that alters the hydrology can make peat soils more vulnerable to fire. When peatlands burn, the fire spreads both above- and belowground. Shrubs and trees provide fuel when lightning strikes and wind blows sparks to life. Peat fires can burn deep into the ground, leaving behind blackened craters where several feet of peat soils have literally gone up in smoke. Once the peat ignites, it creates a slow-burning, smoldering fire that can persist for weeks or months. Peat fires can be stubbornly difficult to extinguish. Although peat is the product of a wet environment, once dried it can be surprisingly resistant to water. Burning peat must be inundated with rainfall or surface flooding, allowing the water enough time to saturate the peat.

One of these peat fires occurred near the Albemarle Sound in eastern North Carolina. On June 1, 2008, the Evans Road fire erupted from a combination of severe drought and summer thunderstorms. A lightning strike triggered a fire on some private farmland where the water table had been lowered through drainage ditches. In four days, the fire grew from seven hundred to twelve thousand acres; by June 14, it had burned more than forty thousand acres. In some areas, the fire burned twenty-four inches deep into the peat soils. Even after the spread of fire was largely contained, the dry peat soils continued to smolder, producing billowing clouds of smoke across the coastal plain. Pollution levels led to Code Purple air quality alerts, warning people to stay indoors. The smoke posed more than a serious health risk; it also represented a massive surge of carbon dioxide into the air. Carbon that had been locked up for centuries was suddenly released, returning to the atmosphere. Scientists estimated the carbon emissions from the Evans Road fire to be almost ten million metric tons—roughly the equivalent of nine coal-fired power plants operating for a year. Fire managers pumped more than two billion gallons of water from lakes and canals to inundate the burning peatlands. When rainfall added much-needed moisture, the fires were finally extinguished in January 2009, seven months after the fire started.

The Evans Road fire was not a unique or isolated event. Much of the same area that burned in 2008 had previously burned in the 1955 Lake Phelps fire, a blaze that covered an estimated 203,000 acres. Later, in 1985, the Allen Road fire was triggered by machinery used for mining the peat soil, eventually burning nearly ninety-five thousand acres in this same area.

One key to why these fires recur is the sheer amount of fuel. The dense shrub bogs and pine woodlands that cover much of the landscape in North Carolina's coastal plain are known as *pocosins*. In a relatively flat landscape, these topographic high points can reach a gentle rise of twelve feet or so, an elevation that indicates deep layers of organic peat. Although pocosin habitat is nutrient-poor and saturated much of the year, the shrubby vegetation is abundant and compact. Thickets of short bay trees, gallberry, and fetterbush, an underbrush carpet of bracken and chain fern—the mosaic of pocosin flora creates an impressive cache of organic matter, all of which is vulnerable to fire.

One early June, I crossed a bridge over the Chowan River and drove south through the heart of the Albemarle–Pamlico Peninsula to Pocosin Lakes National Wildlife Refuge. Hundreds of beachgoers must pass through this area every summer on their way to the Outer Banks, but few of them seemed to be making a detour from Highway 64 to explore the solitude of nature. I traveled with my husband, a keen birder who eyed the shrub bog as an attractive hiding place for warblers. We stopped along the south edge of Lake Phelps, completely hidden from view until we followed a narrow path leading to the shoreline. The large lake has a reputation for good fishing, but not a boat stirred the water on this quiet morning. Heading down a gravel road on foot, we kept our ears open for birds and eyes open for bears. This part of the peninsula hosts one of the largest populations of black bears in the southeastern United States but, like the tourists and fisherfolk, they were not to be seen. The secluded nature of the place was misleading, though; we were not alone. The rising buzzy notes of a prairie warbler kept repeating like a bird going up an escalator. As we ventured farther into the refuge, we heard the persistent chip call of the common yellowthroat, the soft trill of a worm-eating warbler, the weird melody of the white-eyed vireo. Pocosins are characterized by evergreen shrubs, and the impenetrable nature of these bogs makes them ideal habitat for small birds—those moving through on migration paths or species that nest in the hidden depths of the swampy thickets. Scattered pond pines and red maples offer taller perches for great crested flycatchers and eastern kingbirds. Pockets of Atlantic white cedar and wet bay forest attract black-throated green and hooded warblers.

Pocosins are described as either "short" or "tall," words that roughly point to the structure of the vegetation. Short pocosins are dominated by shrubs, often stunted in growth because of the nutrient-poor soils. Tall pocosins have shallower peat layers, and with more available nutrients they support pond pines and higher-canopy shrubs—thus, "tall" vegetation. Intermingled with the peatlands are related varieties of swamp forest along stream margins and bordering lakes. The subtle differences in the shape and character of pocosins have an important effect on the hydrology of the region.

Pocosins are a critical source of freshwater in the coastal ecosystem, influencing the flow of water aboveground and below. In undisturbed pocosins, the water table can rise and fall by as much as three feet between seasons or from dry years to wet years. The pocosins are wetter in winter when plants are dormant and rainfall saturates the soil. In spring, water levels drop as plants awaken and draw up water for growth. In summer and fall, up to 90 percent of water loss is through evapotranspiration, the process by which water moves from plants and soils into the atmosphere. The natural water cycle can be disrupted by short-term events—by fire or drought, and by tropical storms or flooding—but human land use activities cause longer term changes.

North Carolina boasts a large concentration of pocosins—an estimated two million acres—though like many wetlands, much of this area been drained for farming, commercial forestry, and development. The Pocosin Lakes National Wildlife Refuge protects more than a hundred thousand acres of pocosin habitat. When the refuge was established in 1990, more than forty-three thousand acres had been hydrologically altered by historic ditching for agriculture. Restoring the hydrology that supports pocosin habitat has been a priority for refuge managers for more than twenty years. The goal is to keep the peatland wet while still allowing for the natural cycle of wet and dry seasons. The balancing act of the restored system provides water storage in the peat without creating areas of standing water, which would shift the habitat to marshland. To date, more than thirty-seven thousand acres have been restored through the installation and management of water control structures. The rewetting approach to restoration helps keep carbon locked in the saturated peat soils, protecting the value of pocosins as long-term carbon storage. Importantly, restoring the hydrology also reduces the vulnerability of pocosins to wildfire, lessening the risk of a sudden loss of carbon to the atmosphere.

Recognizing the role that pocosins play in sequestering and storing carbon has led to an innovative pilot project in the Clayton Blocks, an area of about twelve hundred acres on the southwest side of the refuge. Through a partnership between the US Fish and Wildlife Service and The Nature Conservancy, the restoration work at Clayton Blocks provided a test case for developing a methodology that can be used to validate, verify, and generate carbon credits in a voluntary carbon market. The Clayton Blocks project led to a protocol approved by ACR (formerly known as the American Carbon Registry) that other landowners can use to develop projects for the sale of carbon credits. The increased amount of carbon stored because of restoration determines the number of carbon credits that can be generated from the project. To meet the requirements of the carbon market, independent measurement and verification must be conducted to ensure that the anticipated carbon benefits are realized. Environmental monitoring before and after the restoration process helps to quantify the project's emission reductions. The Nature Conservancy and TerraCarbon, LLC, a private firm that helps guide the development and sale of carbon credits, developed a plan for the Clayton Blocks project. Carbon markets could offer a strong financial incentive to restore drained and degraded peatlands. With technical support from Duke University Wetland Center, East Carolina University, and the US Geological Survey, the wetland restoration project at Clayton Blocks helps to set a standard practice for other peatland restoration efforts.

Walking along the gravel road through the refuge, I sensed how different this landscape was from the northern peatlands I had explored over the past couple years. The pocosins had a decidedly southern feeling about them. Maybe it was the abundance of flowering shrubs all in their glorious summer bloom. Sweetbay, boasting the classic, creamy white flowers characteristic of its family. Honey-cup, with graceful reddish stems holding clusters of delicate, bell-shaped blossoms. Titi, a prolific shrub in the wettest parts of the pocosin, overhanging the ditches with sprays of ivory flowers that burst open like fireworks. The floral display signals the wealth of nectar to be found here, luring insects that attract birds and, in turn, draw in the bird-watchers like my husband and me.

The heat of the day was building under the cloud cover, and I took a deep drink from my water bottle. Frogs called out like the twang of loose banjo strings. Bees hummed under the dangling honey-cup flowers. Stopping to scan the view, my eyes were drawn to the snags poking up through the dense thicket of shrubs. Some bore black burn scars, reminders of the fire history that has shaped the pocosins. We stood in the heart of where the Evans Road fire had burned a hole in the ground almost fifteen years ago. Now the sweetbay and gallberry had grown compact and shoulder-high, obscuring the hollows left by the fires of the past.

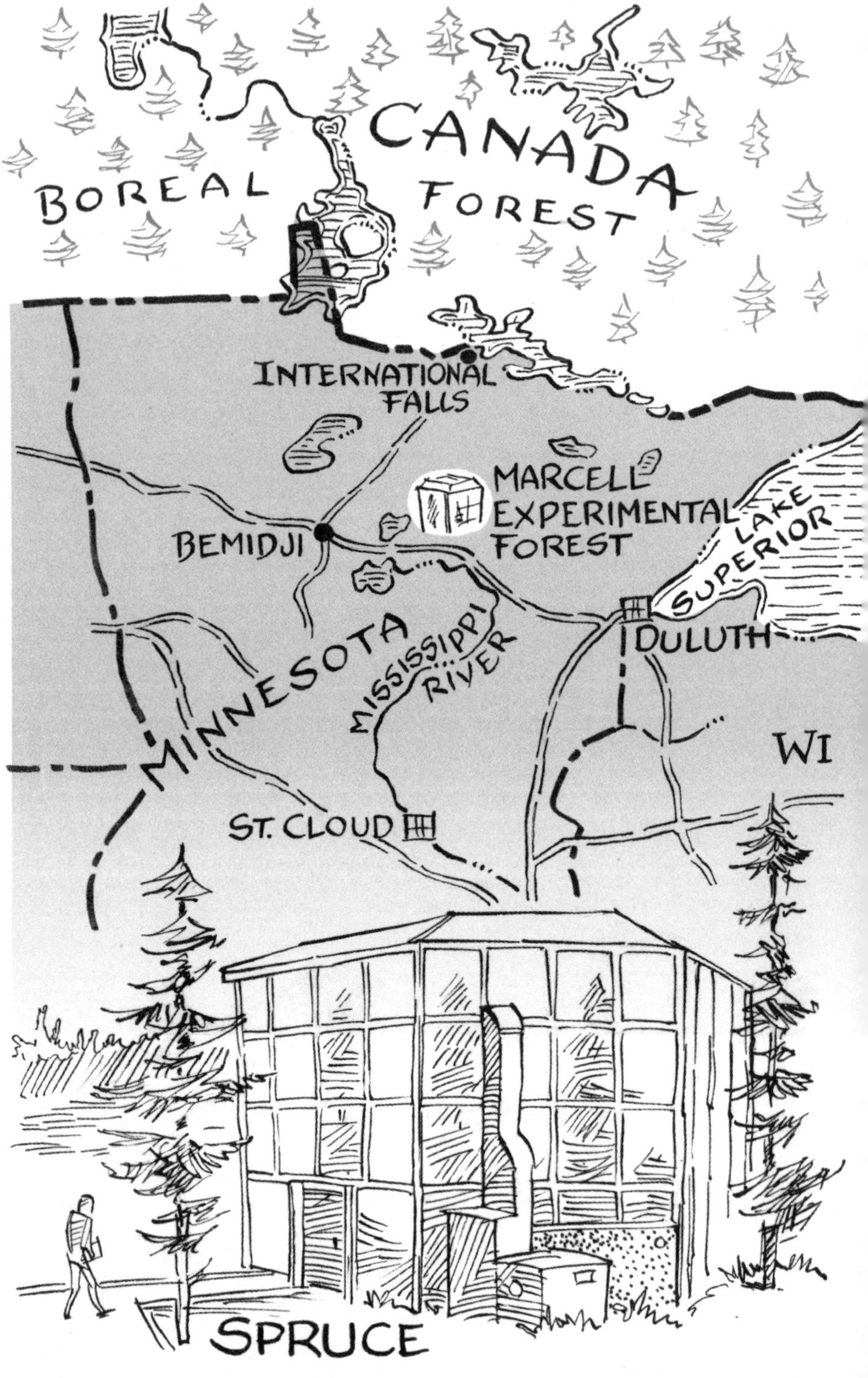
CANADA
BOREAL FOREST
INTERNATIONAL FALLS
MARCELL EXPERIMENTAL FOREST
BEMIDJI
LAKE SUPERIOR
DULUTH
MINNESOTA
MISSISSIPPI RIVER
WI
ST. CLOUD
SPRUCE

EIGHT

Counting Carbon

Marcell Experimental Forest, Minnesota

The world's peatlands and the global climate system are bound together, each influencing the other. Peatlands sequester carbon, absorbing it from the atmosphere and storing it deep in the soil, a process that mitigates the increasing concentration of greenhouse gases in the atmosphere that are driving climate change. At the same time, planetary warming already underway is changing the nature of peatlands, unsettling the flow of water, carbon, and time.

To understand the causes and consequences of climate change, scientists build earth system models to analyze the interactions between the atmosphere, oceans, and terrestrial landscapes. Models are informed by empirical data, but they are simplifications of the real world, a world that is too complex to describe in even the most elegant equations. Still, models are useful and necessary tools to help us comprehend the future of our planet. Global climate models are a bit like pyramids, built on layers of other models that simulate different aspects of earth systems. Land surface models are part of the pyramid, as the world's forests, grasslands, and wetlands all have profound influence on the climate as sinks and sources of greenhouse gases.

Peatlands, however, are often left out of models—an omission that presents a huge knowledge gap, considering that peatlands play an outsized role in the future climate of our planet. Though peatlands cover only about 3 percent of the earth's land surface, they hold as much as one-third of the earth's terrestrial carbon. Climate scientists have wrestled with the problem of integrating peatlands into global climate models for more than a decade. The challenge is diversity: The nature of peatlands varies widely, in both time and space. At a microscale, carbon cycling within a peatland varies from hummocks to hollows. On a broader scale, peat accumulates at different rates under different climatic and hydrological conditions.

Quantifying carbon in peatlands involves estimating the amount of carbon stored in the peat soils and the fluxes of carbon uptake and release. Some climate experts describe the task of counting carbon in terms of a budget, tracking the balance of capital (carbon stock), gains (carbon uptake by plants, stored in peat soils), and losses (release of carbon to the atmosphere). To measure change requires a starting point, a reference. Estimating the amount of carbon held in peatlands starts with knowing the spatial extent of wetlands and discerning which wetlands hold stores of the high-carbon peat. Many countries have, or are developing, inventories of peatlands, based on vegetation and soil maps constructed from field studies and geospatial data. Building an inventory of peatlands for places that are difficult to access, such as the far northern latitudes or the tropics, relies on remote-sensing data. Both "bottom-up" and "top-down" methods of calculating the area and volume of peat come with varying degrees of uncertainty. To get the full picture of a peatland, the measure of its spatial extent is combined with estimates of soil carbon. Think of it as a three-dimensional map, like one you might make of an ocean, an assessment of the area and the depth. In a peatland map, the depth of peat is often unknown, unless field studies have measured it through a series of peat cores. Peatland inventories often use conservative estimates of peat depth (perhaps one to two meters) when many peatlands may hold significantly deeper stores of peat, and thus much larger carbon stocks.

Carbon stored in peat is not immune to change, but changes can be difficult to measure. How much is added to the stored carbon pool through vegetation growth and accumulation of organic matter? How much is lost through decomposition and release of carbon gases to the atmosphere? The point when a peatland shifts from carbon sink to carbon source is critical to understanding how peatlands influence the global climate system and how the climate system in turn affects the carbon stored in peat. Even peatlands that continue to function as carbon sinks may be changing, losing their capacity to store additional carbon and keep it in the ground. Measuring greenhouse gas emissions from peatlands—under a range of conditions, from undisturbed to degraded to restored habitat—is an ongoing focus of field monitoring, modeling, and research.

The calculation of net change in greenhouse gas emissions is complicated by the nature of different forms of gaseous carbon, particularly carbon dioxide (CO_2) and methane (CH_4). Disturbed peatlands produce carbon dioxide in abundance, a by-product of decomposition that occurs when organic material in the peat is exposed to oxygen. All wetlands—including both undisturbed and rewetted peatlands—generate methane. Methane is shorter-lived in the atmosphere but is eighty times more potent than carbon dioxide in trapping heat over a time span of twenty years. Organic soils, and drained peatlands in particular, are also a source of nitrous oxide (N_2O), which has an extreme warming effect on the atmosphere as well as damaging the ozone layer. (Nitrous oxide emissions are more significant in the lower latitudes where tropical fens and swamp forests are being converted to agriculture.) To further complicate the equation, emissions of carbon dioxide and methane are not the only ways in which carbon losses occur in peatlands. Carbon dissolved in water is lost when peat is physically disturbed by water flow. It can be a blowout or a slow leak: Flood events cause short-term losses; erosion and drainage lead to long-term losses. Fires also trigger carbon losses in the form of particulate matter and volatile organic carbon compounds and lead to extreme greenhouse gas emissions.

Current earth system models project a sobering future for peatlands and for the global climate system. As temperatures rise and precipitation patterns change, peatlands are predicted to lose their ability to maintain their long-held stores of carbon. Much of that carbon loss will be in the form of carbon gases, both carbon dioxide and methane. The addition of those greenhouse gases into the atmosphere further amplifies the driving force behind the warming climate, creating a positive feedback loop. Models are complex, however, as they reflect a world full of variation and diversity. Any one component of an integrated model might focus on a particular element in an ecosystem; some are cleverly named, such as the MEND (Microbial Enzyme Decomposition) and the TAM (Transport and Absorptive fine roots and Mycorrhizal fungi) models. The key to improving the accuracy of models is to count everything—any of dozens of variables that can reflect the role of peatlands in the global carbon cycle. As the Russian novelist (and accomplished lepidopterist) Vladimir Nabokov once wrote: “In high art and pure science detail is everything.”

In northern Minnesota, wetland scientists are peering into the future, using a kind of looking glass to understand the effects of climate change in the peatlands of the north woods. In this region—the southern extent of the vast boreal forests that cover much of Canada—temperatures are rising. Winters are warming faster than summers; the growing season, between the last frost in spring and the first frost in fall, has lengthened by three weeks. Shorter, warmer winters present several risks, both ecological and economic. Insect pests are an increasing concern, as milder winters allow more insects to survive the season and offer more hospitable habitat for the spread of new insect pests, such as emerald ash borer. Spring highs and lows have changed, too. Early "false springs" can lead to forests leafing out during warm spells, only to suffer from late spring frosts. These warming trends raise a host of questions about the effects on peatland ecosystems. The vast, wooded bogs of the boreal forest store enormous amounts of carbon, locked away in the peat and thus acting as a carbon sink. As the climate continues to warm, scientists wonder how peatlands will respond.

A couple hours' drive northwest of Duluth, Minnesota, the Marcell Experimental Forest is an ideal site for observing changes in its black spruce and raised bog habitats, typical of peatlands found across northern Minnesota. Marcell is one of eighty-four experimental forests managed by the US Department of Agriculture Forest Service, but one of just a dozen that focus on watershed research. Established in 1960, Marcell Experimental Forest has been the site of hundreds of research projects on environmental conditions that affect forest and peatland ecosystems in this transition zone between boreal and broadleaf deciduous forests. Early research in the 1970s included air deposition studies that informed scientific understanding of acid rain. Marcell Experimental Forest research was also groundbreaking in recognizing the role of freshwater wetlands as sources of methane emissions. Studies here use a paired watershed approach: one control area to one treatment area. Long-term studies that compare changes in paired sites are the gold standard for monitoring environmental influences that occur over time, and they are particularly important for understanding the effects of climate change. The Marcell Research Center and its associated scientists manage six designated research watersheds: S1 through S6. The "S" stands for "swamp"; when Marcell was established in 1960, scientists knew little about peatland ecosystems, considering them all just swamps.

I was fortunate to have the ideal guide: Randy Kolka, a soil scientist for the USDA Forest Service and one of the leading US experts on peatlands. Randy gave up his Labor Day holiday to give me a tour of the research projects that make Marcell Experimental Forest a living laboratory. His office in Grand Rapids, about thirty minutes south of Marcell, was a comfortably large workspace, its walls and shelves cluttered with the signs of a professional life well-lived: photographs of his children and a dozen or so samples of their artwork; photos of the scientist-fisherman proudly holding walleyes as long as his arm; innumerable thank-you cards, news clippings, and certificates of appreciation. On his desk was a can of extra-strength mosquito repellent, a necessity of fieldwork in the north woods.

After a short introduction to the Marcell Research Center, Randy gave me an overview of its most famous research project, SPRUCE, a clever acronym for "Spruce and Peatland Responses Under Changing Environments." The SPRUCE experiment is unique, distinguished by the use of giant open-topped chambers designed for long-term monitoring of the effects of increased temperatures and concentrations of atmospheric carbon dioxide. Monitoring the release of greenhouse gases from each chamber and how they differ under increased warmth or carbon dioxide is a central research question for SPRUCE. The project evolved from a series of earlier experiments known as FACE, for Free Air Carbon Dioxide Enrichment. Starting in the mid-1990s, Oak Ridge National Laboratory and a host of collaborating research institutions began examining the effects of higher carbon dioxide concentrations on a variety of ecosystems. The SPRUCE experiment adds to this knowledge by creating a unique above- and belowground warming temperature treatment. The research project applies these two environmental variables—carbon dioxide and heat—to the poorly understood ecosystem of boreal peatlands. The question of how the changing atmosphere and climate may affect the huge stores of carbon in peatlands is one of far-reaching significance.

We climbed into Randy's Forest Service truck and headed north. We made a few stops along the way, sampling a diversity of peatland habitats and seeing the observation equipment that keeps a continuous watch on the vital signs of these wetlands. The first stop was a large, treeless bog, spreading out as a broad swath of sedges, *Sphagnum* mosses, and low-growing plants. All my peatland favorites were here: Labrador tea, cranberry, bog rosemary, leatherleaf, sundew, pitcher plants. Sedges waved their elegant seed heads above the hummocks and hollows of the surface. To the north, a cluster of bog cotton appeared like a low mist rising from the wetland. A boardwalk led to a collection of monitoring equipment that looked like a weather observation station with some added bells and whistles: enclosed water gauges to measure the rise and fall of the water table, and a small heater in the cabinet housing the equipment, necessary to keep the instruments from freezing in the winter. Upslope, propane tanks would be delivered later in fall to supply the energy and heat.

I asked why this bog is treeless, when so much of the peatland around us is covered in black spruce. Randy explained this site has a very high water table, so close to the surface that the aerated soil layer is not deep enough for trees to establish roots. Even the shrubs that grow thickly here, if pulled up from the peat, would reveal root structures in a broad but shallow network. Below this active layer, each stratum of peat adds weight to the layers below it, sinking the dead plant material into the saturated zone of the peat, where the process of decay and decomposition slows dramatically. Walking back to the upland, I passed through a lagg—the transition zone between the raised bog and forest. Though the topography was almost impossible to discern with the naked eye, this peatland represents a type of domed bog. As these bogs accumulate layers of peat over time, the sheer volume of biomass causes the bog to form a convex surface. Precipitation falling on the domed bog flows downhill to the periphery, where the lagg forms a kind of moat around the bog. Because the lagg receives runoff from both the bog and the surrounding upland, it holds a richer blend of nutrients and minerals, and thus supports a greater diversity of plants and trees that fringe the open bog.

At our next stop, we followed a boardwalk into a quiet retreat wooded with black spruce and tamarack. The trees here are shallow-rooted and vulnerable to wind toss, and more than a few of the slender trunks tilted at odd angles—the reason these are sometimes called "drunken forests." A root mat where a tree toppled over completely showed a lateral mesh of fibrous roots, designed to spread wide but not deep. This bog, Randy told me, is his favorite place on earth. I understood why: The filtered light of the forest, the stillness of the air, the hidden depth of peat below our feet—this is a place where time seems both endless and immediate. A slice of bog heaven.

We arrived at the S1 bog, site of the SPRUCE experiment. At the edge of a wide dirt parking area, a small gate was dwarfed by the structures behind it. The entrance seemed remarkably modest, given the sophisticated engineering that sits behind the low fence. The sign was not a typical billboard of names and logos acknowledging the various agencies and partners that share responsibility for this facility, which would include the USDA Forest Service Northern Research Station and the Department of Energy's Oak Ridge National Laboratory. Instead, the sign simply read "SPRUCE" above a graphic depiction of a conifer tree flanked by two low shrubs under a broad dome. Red and green arrows were labeled "+C" for temperature (Celsius) and "+CO_2" for carbon dioxide. The sign, which Randy had a hand in designing, tells the whole story in a nutshell. The experiment aims to see what happens when you increase temperature and the concentration of atmospheric carbon dioxide, conditions associated with climate change.

The research site was set up like a series of giant open-topped terrariums, each enclosing a piece of forest. We entered one of three pods, each of which has several chambers linked by a boardwalk. The grated walkway is wide enough to accommodate large equipment, perfectly level, and deeply anchored into the peat. A station of instruments surrounding a central tower sits between the chambers and monitors the ambient conditions—temperature, humidity, precipitation, even seed carried by the wind. Measuring these variables outside the chambers is essential to maintaining specific treatment conditions inside of them. Each chamber serves a different role in observing the effects of increased temperature and carbon dioxide concentrations on the peatland environment. Each one is twenty-three feet high, forty-two feet across, and clear so that sunlight can penetrate the enclosure. They are open at the top with the uppermost panels angled slightly inward, a modification to help conserve energy. Maintaining the five heated chambers at temperatures above ambient conditions in both summer and winter requires a lot of energy and carefully calibrated systems.

A sign over the door of a chamber labeled Plot 17 read, "Welcome to a warmer future: +9°C, Ambient CO_2." Unique to the SPRUCE experiment is the subsurface soil heating system: sixty-nine heating tubes inserted into the peat, spaced in a concentric pattern to provide even warmth belowground. Fans inside the chamber blew a continuous breeze of warmed air that is circulated aboveground. The black spruce trees inside Plot 17 showed a scattering of brown needles, likely a sign of heat stress. The tamarack trees are deciduous conifers that would normally turn yellow and lose their needles later in fall; here, they looked like they might drop by late September. The shrub layer was thick and leathery, apparently thriving in the heat, while the *Sphagnum* moss beneath was wilted and fading.

The SPRUCE project offers a powerful method of experimentation and measurement, a means of quantifying the intricate functioning of an ecosystem. This collection of octagonal chambers is both functional and fantastic, filled with an array of devices to measure just about everything that is measurable. But the SPRUCE experiment is more than an impressive assortment of technical equipment: It is a nexus of research institutions, supported by the USDA Forest Service and Oak Ridge National Laboratory. In just ten years, a cadre of research scientists have conducted hundreds of experiments and produced more than 170 peer-reviewed papers that advance the collective understanding of peatland ecosystems and, in particular, how vulnerable their carbon stores are to a changing climate. What is learned through experimentation and observation is applied to earth system surface models, tweaking them to simulate the real world more accurately.

As we followed the walkway that encircles the chamber, Randy described each piece of equipment as a link to a line of inquiry in the multifaceted experiment. Capped pipes of various sizes connected to underground cameras that photograph plant roots, so that growth and condition could be measured. Silvery blankets wrapped around the trunks of several trees enclosed sensors that monitor how the trees respire, drawing up water to support the growth of branches and needles. Small funnel-like cones captured seeds that have fallen from the trees or blown in through the top of the chamber. A sturdy cylinder embedded in the peat served as a collar on which larger equipment could be mounted to measure carbon dioxide, methane, and other gases released from this sample of forest and peatland ecosystem. One of the instruments that caught my attention involved thin metal bands cinched tightly around a tree's main trunk like a decorative arm bracelet. Randy explained that these measure the microscopic change in diameter of the trunks as each expands and shrinks through cycles of respiration—a tool to measure the tree breathing in and out. I considered the way one tree cycles carbon through the seasons and over the course of its lifetime. Now multiply that by the millions of black spruce trees that blanket the circumpolar boreal forest. The collective power of this great exchange—between the peat soil, the forest, and the atmosphere—is vast indeed.

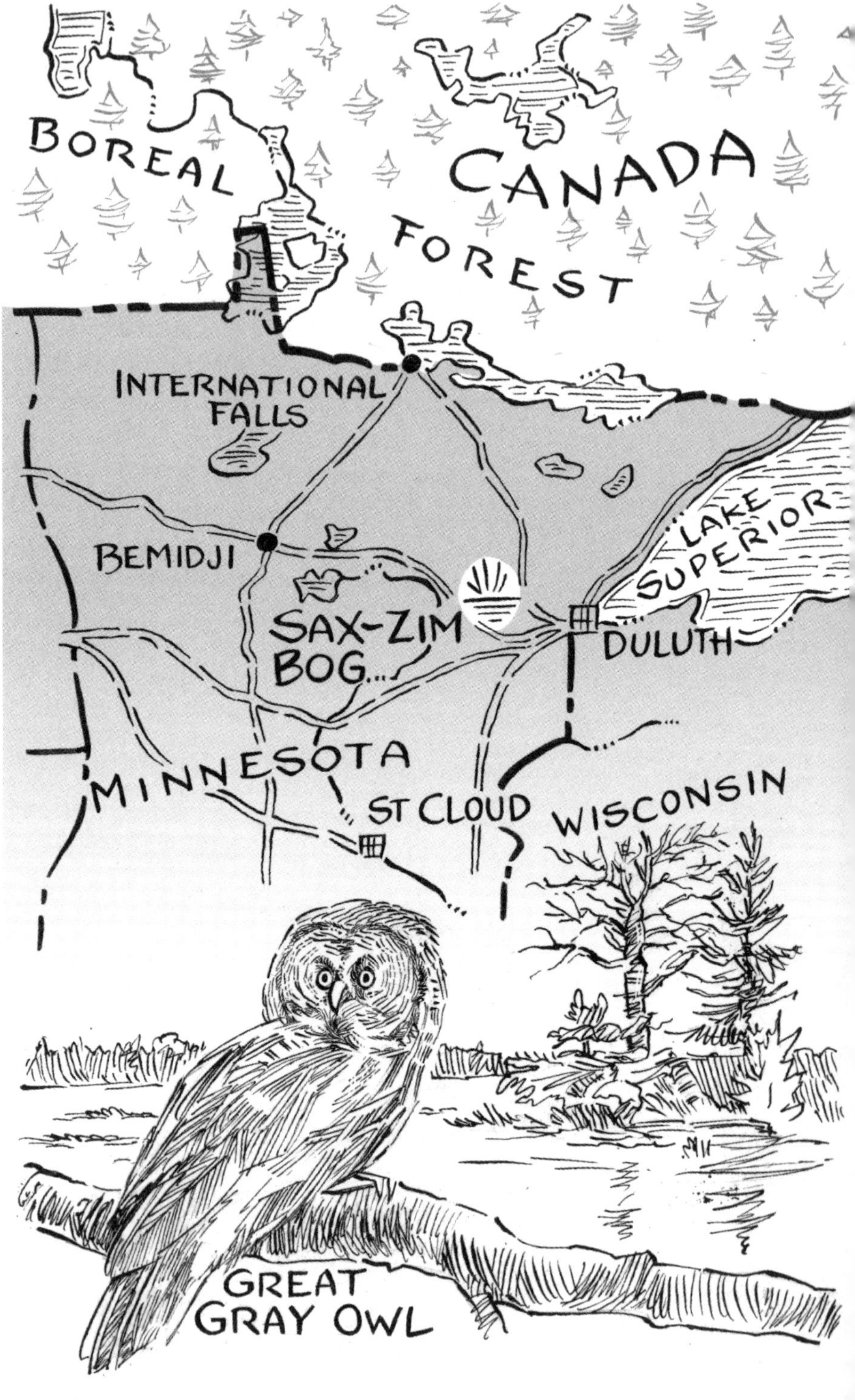
BOREAL
CANADA
FOREST
INTERNATIONAL FALLS
LAKE SUPERIOR
BEMIDJI
SAX-ZIM BOG...
DULUTH
MINNESOTA
ST CLOUD
WISCONSIN
GREAT GRAY OWL

NINE

Recovery

Sax-Zim Bog, Minnesota

The rewards of peatland restoration are potentially huge. Intact and undisturbed, peatlands represent an enormous carbon sink, but drained and degraded peat creates a sizable source of carbon emissions. Scientists estimate that, globally, damaged peatlands release an estimated two gigatons of carbon dioxide each year, about 5 percent of all human-caused greenhouse gas emissions. Stopping the loss of stored carbon achieves an immediate benefit; recovering a peatland's natural ability for carbon uptake delivers an ongoing cumulative benefit.

Restoring drained peatlands can reduce, or even halt, the loss of carbon dioxide. But rewetting peat soils can also increase emissions of methane. Carbon dioxide has a long residence time in the atmosphere, on the order of centuries. Methane lingers for only about twelve years, but during that time, it has a much more potent warming effect than carbon dioxide. The challenge is to understand the net balance of greenhouse gases, in the short and long term. Peatland scientists around the world are wrestling with this question, and the answers may vary with different peatland types in different climatic and geographic settings.

Peatland restoration aims for three things: to reverse the damage of altered hydrology; to reestablish the peatland plant community; and to restart the process of absorbing and storing carbon. Depending on the type of drainage system and the condition of a degraded wetland, the common methods for restoring hydrology are either blocking or filling ditches. The essential first step is rewetting peatlands to restore their hydrological integrity. Blocking drainage ditches is perhaps the most common practice and can be the most cost-effective. The goal is to flip the function of the ditch system from one that moves water away from the peatland to one that keeps water on the land. The low-tech approach is to simply plug the drainage ditches with peat from an adjacent berm. A more engineered technique involves adapting existing water control features such as check dams or weirs. Water management systems can be costly, though, and they require long-term monitoring, repairs, and readjustments. Another option is to completely fill the drainage ditches, restoring the surface elevation and eliminating the drainage system altogether.

A peatland is not just a storage unit of water and carbon; it is a microcosm of life in all its mystery and complexity. Rewetting degraded peatlands opens the door to recovery of the plant community that thrives in these unique wetlands. But time alone does not heal all wounds. Even when soils are sufficiently saturated, many peatland plants do not successfully come back on their own. Mosses and sedges need a high water table—just five to ten inches below the surface—but soil moisture is not the only factor for successful restoration. Soil structure is also important; compaction of peat resulting from drainage, fire, grazing animals, or vehicle use can damage the soil pores necessary for water storage and transport through the peat. Water chemistry matters, too. Polluted runoff from agriculture and roadways can raise nutrient and salt concentrations; atmospheric deposition of industrial pollutants, such as nickel and copper from smelting, create physiological stress for peat plants.

The chances for restoration depend, in part, on the nature of the damage. In some drained peatlands, vegetation persists but has become dominated by plant species suited to drier habitat. In peatlands that have been drained and excavated, there may not be enough remaining plant material—no mosses, no sedges, and no seed bank—to recolonize those species in the exposed peat. For restoration to succeed, some management intervention may be necessary.

Small-scale revegetation of peatlands attempts to replant native species. Various methods include introducing seeds, seedlings, or plant cuttings collected from nearby peatlands. On a larger scale, a technique known as "moss layer transfer" has been widely practiced in Canada, especially on peatlands used for commercial harvesting of peat. The process can transform a bare surface of scraped peat soil into a growing layer of vegetation. First comes the sprinkling of moss fragments collected from a donor site. The extraction of a thin moss layer from a healthy area of mosses and relocation to another is a bit like a skin graft, with the intent of having the introduced material take hold. The process also requires blocking drainage ditches to raise the water table and restore the hydrological condition of the site. Over time the transplants become established, expanding to form a lush moss carpet, which serves as foundation for other peatland species to follow. The moss layer transfer technique has been tested for more than twenty years and proven to be fairly successful in establishing a healthy carpet of *Sphagnum* within a decade of restoration, and in some cases in just three to five years. Establishing a layer of living *Sphagnum* is obviously an improvement over bare earth but is only the beginning of recovery for a degraded peatland.

Ecological restoration can be measured by plant diversity as a proxy. But another important way to gauge the success of restoration is whether and when the ecosystem begins to resume the accumulation of peat—and to determine whether the restored peatland shifts from a carbon source to a carbon sink. Factoring in the variable greenhouse gas fluxes makes this a tricky equation. In a study published in 2020, a team of peatland scientists in Germany compared carbon dioxide and methane emissions over time in restored peatlands. Given the difference in long-term versus short-term effects of the two gases, the study estimated cumulative emissions under several different scenarios based on the timing and extent of restoration. Their results emphasize the importance of restoring peatlands sooner than later. The study concluded that avoiding the continued carbon dioxide emissions from degraded peatlands has a net climate benefit despite the uptick in methane emissions. Restoration is not a quick fix but demands patience and commitment. The benefits are realized over decades and centuries, and only if the peatland remains intact and protected from future damage.

The challenging work of restoration is largely in the hands of scientists, researchers, conservationists, and volunteers, all driven by a sense of urgency and a deep curiosity to understand the dynamic nature of peatlands. Long-term ecological recovery of peatlands is more than a matter of "just add water," though this is a powerful start to the process. As geologist Marcia Bjornerud writes in her book *Timefulness*, "The carbon conundrum is not the only environmental challenge of our time, but it underscores a more general, obstinate fact: that there is an immense asymmetry in the time it takes to consume, alter, or destroy natural phenomena compared with the time required to replace, restore, or repair them."

The first time I visited Sax-Zim Bog, I savored its fragrance. Along the margin of a sedge meadow the late summer smells of damp earth and dry bracken ferns filled the air. Moving from open sunlight into the shady woods there was a change in the atmosphere, like stepping into a cool bath. Dappled light through the trees created a kind of enchanted forest, charged with the tangy aroma of black spruce and tamarack. Above me, a pair of Canada jays flitted from one tree to another, finding food to eat and to cache for colder times ahead. White-winged crossbills perched higher in the spruces, while red-breasted nuthatches scurried up and down the tree trunks in midcanopy. Dead trees had flakes of bark piled at the base, evidence of a black-backed woodpecker foraging for grubs. Invisible in the hush of the forest, owls kept silent in the treetops, waiting for dusk.

Sax-Zim Bog lies in the center of Glacial Lake Upham, a legacy of the Pleistocene that formed as ice sheets receded and meltwaters drained through a series of outlets to Glacial Lake Duluth. Those glacial remnants are now a series of boggy areas across the headwaters of the St. Louis River basin and its tributaries. This is a land of forested peatlands, the southern edge of a vast boreal ecosystem that covers more than half of Canada. Like much of Minnesota, the area around Sax-Zim Bog has been dissected by roads and ditches in a grid pattern, creating a patchwork of farm fields, woods, and peatlands. A nonprofit group, the Friends of Sax-Zim Bog, has protected a collection of parcels since 2011 that now total more than four thousand acres—a small but important slice of the Sax-Zim Bog landscape that spans three hundred square miles. In addition to black spruce and tamarack bog, the preserve includes a variety of habitat types: upland maple forest, willow-alder thickets, sandy pine woods, and floodplain forests.

This diversity attracts birds that favor black spruce bogs, such as the great gray owl, a forest bird that requires open habitats for supplying its winter diet of meadow voles. Some birds found here, like the boreal chickadee, are known as bog specialists that are typically found much farther north. As a result, Sax-Zim Bog has become something of a mecca for bird-watchers and is part of a designated Important Bird Area. In winter, at least five thousand people visit the preserve, willing to brave the cold to find a treasure like a Northern Hawk Owl. Spring birding is rewarding too, with 120 species known to nest here, including 20 species of warblers.

I spent the day with Clinton Dexter-Nienhaus, head naturalist for Friends of Sax-Zim Bog, a man with an encyclopedic knowledge of the preserve's biodiversity. Clinton has compiled a list of over 3,000 plant, animal, and insect species, including more than 117 species of ferns and mosses and 600 species of moths. And the list continues to grow, as each year the Friends of Sax-Zim Bog host a "bio-blitz," an event that harnesses the skills and enthusiasm of volunteers and experts to record every species they can find—not only birds, but lichens, fungi, butterflies, dragonflies, reptiles, and amphibians.

Late in the afternoon, the stillness of the forest inspired me to lay down in a deep cushion of moss. It was a heavenly feeling, being nestled in the living surface of the peat. I breathed deeply, thinking "if only I could put this in a bottle." As it turns out, someone has. A forester from Minneapolis, under the trade name of Forester John, creates essential oils with the signature tree species found in national parks like Acadia, Denali, and Olympic. Each blend of oil captures the scent of those iconic forests. For Sax-Zim Bog, Forester John uses a combination of black spruce and tamarack, the keystone trees of the boreal forest. Months later, while sequestered at home during the pandemic, I would revisit the bog by inhaling a whiff of that distilled forest air.

Minnesota is blessed with an abundance of peatlands—as much as seven million acres, according to recent soil data—largely concentrated in a swath across the northeastern and north-central part of the state. Wetlands in the Midwest, including peatlands, are a legacy of the glacial past, but not all of them have survived the twentieth century's zeal for ditching and drainage. To the south and west, most of the prairie and wetland habitats have been drained and converted to highly productive farmland. But northern Minnesota's extensive peatlands proved to be a disappointment to promoters of the agricultural dream. Despite vigorous ditching campaigns, the wet soils were hard to till and harder to tame. Efforts to farm these northern peatlands were largely abandoned, but the imprint of the ditch network has had lasting effects.

Even after a century, ditched peatlands have not fully healed on their own. Some peatlands are still physically and ecologically intact and continue to support native vegetation, but drainage ditches have altered the hydrology by lowering the water table, allowing oxygen to seep deeper into the peat surface along the ditches. As a result, the chemical and biological processes of oxidation and decomposition accelerate, breaking down the organic matter that has accumulated in the peat over millennia and releasing carbon into the atmosphere or downstream. The damage, however, may be reversible. In Minnesota, an estimated six hundred thousand acres of peatlands are affected by drainage, with varying degrees of impact, but are not actively being farmed or grazed. Restoring the ecological function of these wetlands holds great promise.

Four years after my first visit, I returned to Sax-Zim Bog to join a group of ecologists on a field visit to research sites in the peatlands, where monitoring is underway to measure the flow of greenhouse gases in restored and unrestored parts of the bog. My hosts are part of a coalition of conservation partners who are assessing the potential to restore Minnesota's damaged peatlands. Given the extent of the state's wetlands and varying degree of impacts, getting a handle on the situation is no small feat. A systematic approach is needed to understand which restoration methods are most effective and where the opportunities are greatest. Scientists with The Nature Conservancy, working with the University of Minnesota, state and federal agencies, and private organizations, are trying to understand what are the most feasible ways to keep carbon in the ground. Protecting and restoring peatlands is a strategy the Conservancy promotes as a "natural climate solution," a potentially cost-effective approach to addressing climate change through land management actions that help ecosystems do what comes naturally to them: absorb and store carbon.

The partners (a self-described "Team Peat") have embarked on a research project by creating a composite map of the state's peatlands, using a suite of data layers for soils and vegetation types. In the first phase of the project, the base map is detailed with additional attributes that factor into the condition of the habitat, such as existing drainage ditch networks and areas of managed forest. Practical considerations, such as ownership and current land use, also contribute to assessing the opportunities for restoration. Initial estimates identified an estimated 450,000 acres of restorable peatlands, and about half of these acres are in public ownership. As the spatial view of the peatland landscape comes into focus, the partners consider conservation strategies that align with the condition of the habitat. Intact peatlands are a priority for protection, as a preventive approach to avoiding the impacts of drainage. Peatlands that are partially drained—affected by historic ditching but not fully converted to agriculture or forestry—are viewed for potential rewetting. The most damaged peatlands may require more intensive actions to restore to functioning ecosystems; drained and converted peatlands may still be recoverable with rewetting to raise the water table and additional efforts to establish keystone plant species, such as *Sphagnum*.

The second phase of work is a complex effort to quantify the potential climate benefits of peatland restoration. In Minnesota, Team Peat has boots on the ground to conduct a detailed comparison of two peatlands: one drained and unrestored, the other a formerly drained site that was rewetted in 2015 as part of a wetland mitigation banking project. The two sites were first surveyed to record the soil pH and plant community characteristics. Over a five-month field season, the team collected measurements of gas fluxes, soil moisture, and groundwater levels. A key element of the study is the depth to water table and how it changes when ditch-blocking is used to restore the hydrology of the peatland.

On a cloud-covered morning I met up with the research crew, led by Kristen Blann and Mark Felice from The Nature Conservancy, at a study site near Meadowlands, south of the Sax-Zim Bog preserve. We hiked in from the road, on a path that leads to a network of monitoring stations. Mark gave a demonstration of the equipment used for measuring greenhouse gas exchanges at the monitoring sites. A LI-COR gas analyzer, about the size of carry-on luggage, connects to a portable chamber resembling a space suit helmet. The chamber is fitted tightly onto a plastic collar set into the peat. Once the chamber is attached and closed, the analyzer measures the concentrations of carbon dioxide and methane being released from the soil. The gas flux collars are spaced at interval distances from the nearest drainage ditch. Water monitoring wells are also placed throughout the study area. The collected data can then be used to compare depth of water table and greenhouse gas measurements relative to the distance from the drainage ditch.

An important focus of the research is to identify the drivers of variability in gas fluxes across the peatland. The LI-COR method of monitoring greenhouse gases has the advantage of specificity, recording gas fluxes at a fine scale. The downside is that peatlands are variable landscapes, with undulating topography and a range of microhabitats. There may be "hot spots" and "cold spots" in gas fluxes, influenced by many factors. Another study led by the University of Minnesota will apply a different methodology for measuring greenhouse gas fluxes, gathering atmospheric data with instruments called eddy covariance towers. These tower systems measure the net transfer of carbon dioxide and methane between the peatland and the atmosphere, giving a larger-scale picture of the peatland's function as either a carbon sink or carbon source. These studies are both designed to understand how a drained peatland compares to a restored peatland. What is learned could inform future restoration projects and help to quantify the potential for peatland recovery.

As we walked back to the road, I looked down the long, narrow trench that drains the wetland. The water is tea-colored, tinted by the organic compounds from the peat, illustrating the loss of dissolved carbon into the water compounding the emissions of carbon dioxide into the air. Drainage changes the chemistry of surface water in other ways. Exposed peat soils can also release mercury, the legacy of atmospheric deposition from coal-burning and other sources. In an aquatic environment, that mercury can be transformed into methylmercury, a potent neurotoxin that accumulates in the ecosystem's food chain. One of the questions for researchers here and at other peatland sites is whether restoring the natural hydrology of the peatland will help to reduce the release of methylmercury into downstream waters.

This parcel was selected for the monitoring project to serve as a sample of peatland that is affected by drainage ditches but not otherwise disturbed; the native bog vegetation is still largely intact. By contrast, the neighboring lands along Highway 8 offered a glimpse of peat mining operations in the area: flattened fields of chocolate brown, flanked by mounds of shredded peat. There is a good reason the peat moss industry is considered "mining." The processes used for removing and processing peat are highly mechanical. The most common method today is vacuum harvesting, which requires specialized equipment to dig drainage ditches around the extraction site, remove surface vegetation, disk the top few inches of peat and form windrows for drying, and finally, vacuum up the dried peat in a tractor-pulled machine that functions somewhat like a giant wet/dry vac. The process may be repeated annually, each time skimming an inch or two of peat. When the upper layer of peat is removed, dried, and shredded, *Sphagnum* is widely marketed as soilless potting mixes for the nursery trade and home gardener, and as a soil supplement for commercial agriculture.

Our next stop on the tour was to visit a restored peatland where a similar suite of monitoring stations is collecting data for comparison to the drained site. We drove north on Highway 7, stopping at the Zim Wildlife Management Area, and headed out into field as the late afternoon light slanted through the clouds. Hiking to the monitoring station was decidedly wetter than our morning walk. The hummocky ground was thick with sedges and moss, dotted with clusters of bog birch. This peatland is in a slow but steady recovery following a restoration effort here eight years ago. The site is part of Lake Superior Wetland Bank; covering twenty-three thousand acres, it is considered one of the largest wetland mitigation banks in the United States. Under Minnesota's Wetland Conservation Act, passed in 1991, development activities that will damage wetlands must either avoid or mitigate those impacts through a regulatory mechanism that aims to achieve "no net loss" of wetlands. Guided by the state's Board of Water and Soil Resources, wetland restoration projects and mitigation banking programs provide a means for developers to comply with permit requirements. When a permit is issued for a project that will harm wetlands, the developer must offset the damage through a wetland restoration project—either conducting their own project (to standards set by regulation), or by purchasing credits from a wetland mitigation bank. There are exemptions to these requirements, though, including maintenance of drainage systems that have been in place for more than twenty-five years. Still, Minnesota does better than most midwestern states in having a strong legal framework for protecting wetlands.

After exchanging farewells with the Team Peat members, I headed back south, stopping at the Warren Nelson Bog, one of the Sax-Zim Bog preserve parcels. As afternoon turned to early evening, the clouds darkened to a milky blue. The forecast for rain was good for the peatland, but I was disappointed that the sky was too overcast to see the rise of the harvest moon that evening. The feel of autumn was in the air, as tamaracks were beginning to turn golden and early fall rain had revived the deep *Sphagnum* moss beds carpeting the forest floor. I reflected on the complexity of ecosystems and the daunting effort of restoring habitats that have been damaged, drained, and dissected into ever smaller pieces. Recovery takes time, but more importantly it takes hundreds of small interactions—between the soil and the sky, between living organisms. Like nature, a peatland is more than the sum of its parts.

PART IV

time

LAKEFILL PROCESS

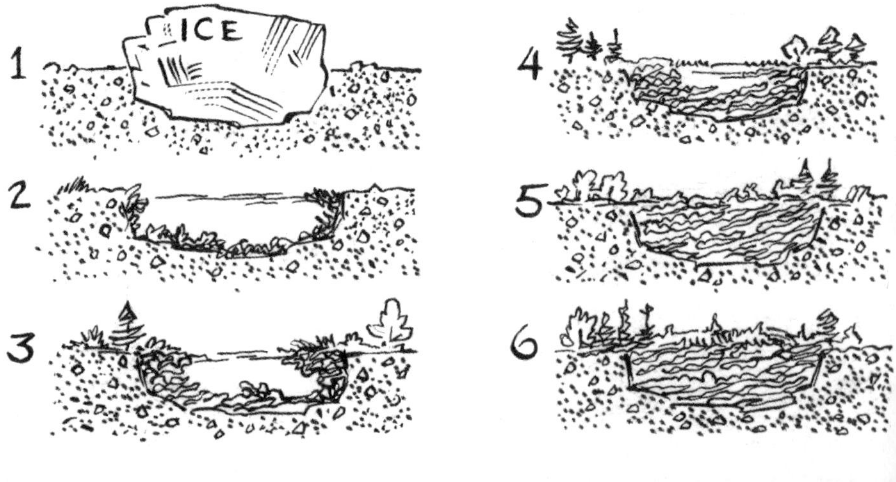

TEN

Climate Past

Kettle Moraine, Wisconsin

"Time the destroyer is time the preserver." A line by T. S. Eliot from his poem *The Four Quartets* would serve as a fitting caption to a biography of peat. The life of plants growing at the surface is followed by death, decay, and burial: layer upon layer of leaves, stems, and roots sinking into the peat that deepens year by year. It seems a steady, slow progression—each spongy page laid down in one growing season after another. In practice, though, the accumulation of peat can occur episodically rather than incrementally. Kettle bogs offer an example. These peatlands are offspring of the last glacial period, formed as ice sheets receded. Mammoth chunks of frozen water, mixed with sand and gravel, were left scattered in the glaciers' wake. The movement of ice sheets also sculpted the landscape; where ice chunks rested in topographic low spots, lakes formed as the ice melted, opening the way for plants to become established in and around the lakes.

The development of a kettlehole bog roughly follows a process known as lake-fill, or *terrestrialization.* A pond forms in a glacial depression where an impermeable layer, such as clay, holds the water left behind by the melting remnant of ice. Over time, sedges and other wetland plants grow around the shoreline, adding layers of organic matter as they die. Root systems form an intricate mesh reaching farther into the pond. Each season of plant growth encroaches into the water, eventually covering the surface with floating mats of vegetation. As the layer of plant life thickens and matures, it can eventually support shrubs and then trees. The slow-motion version of kettle peatland creation depicts *Sphagnum* moss gradually covering the lake surface as vegetation encroaches inward from the lake edge, transforming the lake to a bog over thousands of years.

Studies of kettle bogs in the upper Midwest, however, suggest that peatland development does not necessarily occur at a leisurely, measured pace. By examining sediment cores from kettle lakes underlain with peat, ecologists Alex Ireland, Robert Booth, Sara Hotchkiss, and Jennifer Schmitz recorded historic changes in plant species that coincided with changing water levels. Through this research, a new conceptual model is emerging that could explain how climatic variability drives peatland growth in intermittent pulses. Their findings showed that extreme drought conditions triggered sudden shifts in ecosystems, from lake to bog—a process that occurred more rapidly than the conventional model of peatland formation. They hypothesized that during and following extended droughts, sedges and other wetland plants expand into the lakebed as water levels drop and more shoreline is exposed. When wetter conditions prevail and lake levels rise, the pioneering plants are uprooted, creating a floating platform for mosses to colonize. This in turn creates the conditions for peat to develop, and the kettle lake transforms to a bog in decades rather than millennia—though a remnant lake may still be visible, like an open window to the past.

Understanding the processes at work in the past to create the peatlands that exist today sheds light on how these wetlands originate and spread. This research involves a kind of reading the tea leaves. Due to the acidic, anaerobic, and saturated nature of peat, plant debris (leaves, seeds, and especially pollen) are preserved at various stages of partial decomposition. This allows scientists with sharp eyes and serious patience to identify the plant fossils in the peat and decipher what species lived in the fen or bog ages ago, as layer after layer of plant material accumulated on the surface. Some of the smaller bits of organic material may have traveled some distance, by wind or water, before being deposited in the kettle. Thus, the story is both local and regional. Ecologist Sara Hotchkiss describes this as "the ecosystem itself writing history in drizzles of detritus." As scientists examine core samples, "sampling down into the peat reveals the story back into time—or the other way, with the story accumulating over time as new peat grows at the top of the profile."

Peatlands are shaped by seasons of weather and decades of climate. The combination of temperature and precipitation determines whether there is more or less water available for life—plants, animals, fungi, bacteria. Gains in an ecosystem water budget (from rain and snow, inflowing streams, rising groundwater) are offset against losses from evaporation, transpiration of water through plants, outlet flows of surface runoff, and falling groundwater. Globally speaking, the amount of water does not increase or decrease but changes form, shifting between atmospheric water vapor to rain and snow. During long stretches of Earth's history, when vast amounts of freshwater were bound up in ice, plants and animals had to cope with conditions of both extreme cold and extreme dry.

Across the northern latitudes, many peatlands have a shared origin story: the end of the Pleistocene. The warming planet released water in trickles and floods, saturating and scouring the landscape. The Ice Age is an important backdrop to the story of peatlands in North America. Yet the creation of peatlands and their advance across the land was not a process that sprang to life only at the end of the Pleistocene epoch. True, many northern latitude peatlands began to form following the "last glacial maximum," the most recent extent of ice sheets some twenty thousand years ago. But the great Ice Age did not keep the world persistently frozen for 2.5 million years. Glacial advances alternated with interglacial periods of milder temperatures, when ice sheets were absent from much of the Northern Hemisphere. We are, in fact, currently living in an interglacial period, the Holocene. The last interglacial period, called the Eemian, lasted from about 130,000 to 115,000 years ago. There is evidence of peatland formation during this warmer and wetter period, and when the climate cooled and glaciers advanced south again, much of this peat was buried—by mineral sediments washing out from the margins of ice sheets, and by the glacial ice itself. Even in the unglaciated lower latitudes, some peatlands were covered by deposits of blown sand or coastal sediments.

Too much or too little water can alter the nature of a peatland or, perhaps, be its genesis. Terrestrialization is one pathway through which peatlands can form by infilling ponds and lakes, as illustrated by the kettle bogs of the upper Midwest. Another mechanism of peatland development is *paludification,* an outward expansion of peat as *Sphagnum* mosses encroach on waterlogged mineral soils. In North America, paludification resulted in the spread of peatlands across a broad swath of the boreal north. Interpreting the past, by reading the stories of peatlands through their buried pages, we see that both pathways have been at work for millennia, creating a dazzling variety of bogs and fens, mires and muskeg. Looking to the future, new lines of inquiry arise. How will shifts in water and temperature influence existing peatlands—shrinking or expanding their range, or changing the character of vegetation? Will they become relics of the past as the world warms? Revisiting T. S. Eliot's poem bears another truth: "Time present and time past / are both perhaps present in time future."

Early autumn has a time-bending quality, a way of slowing each day as the lingering warmth of summer mingles with the impending chill of winter. Mornings come later, and dusk sooner. The sun, at its lowering angle, appears to be slipping away, over the horizon and into the past. It was in mid-October that I traveled to Wisconsin to get a sense of the glacial history that underlies peatlands across the northern latitudes. The climate has warmed since the end of the Pleistocene, and with it the landscape of the upper Midwest has shifted from tundra to forest to prairie. The fauna has changed as well as the flora; the great beasts of the Ice Age are gone, and humans have filled almost every ecological niche. But there is still evidence of the great forces that shaped this landscape, and much of it is visible on the Ice Age Trail—a network of footpaths that crosses the state tracing the margin of ice from the last glacial period, aptly named the Wisconsin glaciation. Hiking a piece of the trail, and exploring to the north and south, I found remnants of the Ice Age past scattered between farms and woodlots, small towns, and rural roads.

One silver-clouded morning, I started from the trailhead at Butler Lake and climbed a set of steps up to the crest of Parnell Esker. Eskers are one of the signature glacial features found across Wisconsin, along with kames, kettles, and moraines. Eskers like Parnell are ridges of sand and gravel formed in ice tunnels during the Pleistocene; as the great ice sheets began to melt, water from the surface moved through these channels, carrying sediment and debris washed from the surface. After the ice made its final retreat, the accumulated rock and sand once buried within the ice was left standing above the surrounding landscape. I was walking on what was once a buried streambed.

The trail climbed and dipped along the winding ridge, and with every stride the rounded cobbles made a pleasant clinking underfoot. I tried to imagine how this world might have felt in the early days, before the forest grew up in the path of glaciers. Scientists estimate the global average temperatures of the Ice Age were about ten degrees Fahrenheit colder than the average temperatures of today. The climate then was also drier, and I would have been exposed to bitter currents of air that swept unimpeded across the rugged terrain. On this mild morning in the twenty-first century, the air was soft, gently cool, and fragrant under the lush canopy of maples and hickories. I was comfortably snug, wrapped in rain gear and sheltered by the trees. Pine trees were audible as a light stirring of wind moved through their branches. I hiked for an hour or so before stopping to pour myself a cup of tea from my thermos, the fragrance of Earl Grey blending with the autumn air. Even with the overcast sky, the forest was full of color. Little wonder that Thoreau called October the "month of painted leaves."

I heard the rain before I felt it. The wind shifted from a sigh to a huff, like the sound made by a startled deer. The rain fell with an echo: first the sound of droplets on leaves in the trees above, then a second falling, splashing against the speckled layers of leaves spread across the ground. The pattering became a pulse, a drumbeat, a waterfall. It alternated between a sound like a river in a shallow riffle and pure whitewater. Then I could see the rain suffusing the landscape with its magical beauty. The shine of water on fallen leaves, a shimmering gleam of color so vivid it can almost be blinding, like tears rising in your eyes. A patch of sumac flamed crimson, a maple leaf curled like the palm of a hand holding a silver pool. Keeping my head down, I noticed things that I might have passed by, unseeing. The spotted salamander traversing wet leaves, a sleeping bee curled under a spray of late-blooming asters. This was a lush, wet world I was passing through.

A lot can change in twenty thousand years. Over the long span of the Pleistocene, as ice sheets pushed across the land in repeated movements of advance and retreat, the surface was reshaped—scraped and scoured here, heaped with rock and sand there. Chunks of ice broke away as the glacial edges thinned and pulled northward, left behind as stranded icebergs on the barren ground. Meltwater laden with silt and gravel washed out across the margins of the retreating glacier, burying these ice blocks and effectively insulating them from rapid melting. In time, with further warming of the climate, the entombed ice turned to liquid and the rock layers that covered them collapsed into the depressions left behind. These potholes created by ice remnants produce glacial features called kettles. Many kettles formed lakes and ponds as they filled with water originating from the melted ice chunk and from the outpouring of meltwater from the retreating glacier. Of the roughly fifteen thousand lakes that now exist in present-day Wisconsin, about two-thirds were formed as kettles.

The advancing ice spread into the basins of Lake Superior and Lake Michigan; in between, the ice pushed forward in six major lobes. Two of these lobes—the Lake Michigan lobe to the east, and the Green Bay lobe to the west—moved toward each other, squeezing their load of silt and rock between them. The power of moving ice churned the underlying surface and carried enormous quantities of rock, from mammoth-sized boulders to fine sand. The jumble of silt and stone was left in the track of the retreating glaciers as a series of ridges known as the Kettle Moraine.

The Kettle Moraine is more than an interesting collection of geological features; it embodies the history of the living landscape as it has changed since the ice retreated. During the Wisconsin glaciation, tundra covered much of the region just south of the ice. Lichens, sedges, and a few resilient grasses and flowering plants made a sparse covering over rocky ground. The soil remained frozen in deep permafrost, with only the surface thawing during brief summers. The cooling and warming cycles of glacial and interglacial periods created an ebb and flow of plant species. As the climate began to warm, spruce trees crept northward into the once-treeless tundra, creating a swath of forest along the edge of glacial lakes. In halting steps, forward and back, the ice sheets finally withdrew from northern Wisconsin about ten thousand years ago. Plant species that had retreated far to the south began to migrate into the northern lands, newly exposed and bare. Kettles, in some places, became isolated wetlands, filling with sedges and mosses, forming pockets of plant communities from earlier, colder times. Many kettle bogs are part of larger wetland systems interlaced with fens and swamp forests. Each kettle is a memoir of its own unique story, from the Pleistocene to the Holocene. Hiking in the Kettle Moraine, and feeling the topography through my feet, I could sense the evolution of the landscape. From the rocky path along Parnell Esker, I headed to the lowlands to find bogs and fens nestled in the kettleholes of the glacial past.

My first excursion into Cedarburg Bog resulted in a bog blowout, a humbling lesson on the hazards of solo travel in peatlands. It was a Sunday afternoon. I had just arrived in Wisconsin and drove straight from Milwaukee westward, seeking a public access point into the bog. Parking across the road from the trailhead, I followed a short path to a boardwalk to the edge of Mud Lake, the largest of six lakes found in the Cedarburg basin. I could see only a slender portion of the lake—a small appendix of open water, quiet and still except for a faint ripple made by some coots making a wary retreat into the surrounding cattail marsh. I retraced my steps and looked for another route that might lead me deeper into the shrubby wetland surrounding the lake. Wearing muck boots, I felt prepared to investigate a muddy path that led toward a reedy thicket. Within a few steps my left foot sunk in up to my knee, and I was held fast by the suction of bog water that began to seep into the top of my waterproof boot. Luckily, I had solid footing on my right side, and a place to sit down where I could pull my foot free of the boot and then wrestle the boot from the sodden peat. I needed to find another route into the bog, and a pair of dry pants.

Cedarburg Bog is a big place. It is the largest intact peatland in southeastern Wisconsin, set in a glacial basin some three and a half miles across and one and a half miles wide. More than two thousand acres are protected as part of the State Natural Area system and as a field station and research area managed by the University of Wisconsin–Milwaukee. Somewhere in this large complex of bog, fen, meadow, and marsh, I figured there must be other ways to enter and explore. The University Field Station is open by permission, with staff- or volunteer-guided walks led by the Friends of Cedarburg Bog. I was lucky. On short notice, John O'Donnell kindly offered a personal tour of the university-managed research reserve, following a boardwalk loop built to provide access to students and researchers.

At the start of the trail, we studied a large aerial photo of the site. John pointed out that Cedarburg Bog sits in a large, irregular bowl, the imprint of a lakebed formed some twelve thousand years ago. The basin has an uneven surface, as small islands of glacial till rise slightly above shallow lowlands. We were heading downhill through a shrubby moat that rings the perimeter of the ancient lake, dense with willows, dogwoods, and sumac. Thickets like this are woven throughout the landscape at Cedarburg. Known as a shrub *carr* (from an old Norse word for brushwood), these plant communities are transitional habitats between sedge meadows and forest.

Cedarburg is not a typical bog but can more accurately be described as a mixture of fen, sedge meadow, and string bog. The peatlands are part of a larger wetland ecosystem, a blend of submerged and emergent aquatic habitats, cattail marsh, shrub carr, and swamp hardwood and conifer forest. Something for everyone, I mused, and John agreed that the ecological diversity of Cedarburg Bog is part of what makes it a valued area for research. A dozen species of birds and more than thirty plants found here are at the southern edge of their range in Wisconsin. The variety and extent of wetland and upland provide food and shelter for an assortment of mammals, including red-backed voles, mink, otters, coyotes, raccoons, opossum, and deer. Their presence was made evident by small piles of scat along the boardwalk. Between the shrub thicket and woods there is ample nesting habitat for swamp sparrows, song sparrows, red-winged blackbirds, common yellowthroats, yellow warblers, and willow flycatchers.

Following a slight rise, we crossed the "west island," an upland swath of black cherry, aspen, and basswood. This high ground was dominated by beech-maple forest before being cut over in the 1940s. We passed through swamp hardwood-conifer forest, where the vivid green of fresh tamarack needles shone in contrast to dead snags. Some of those snags were remnants of black ash trees decimated by emerald ash borer, an invasive beetle killing ash trees across North America. Other hardwoods have come and gone from this forest. American elm trees once grew here before they were wiped out by a fungal pathogen, Dutch elm disease.

Logging, pests, and diseases are not the only disruptions to an ecosystem; the dominant species of one age may give way to another with changes in wet and dry conditions, rise and fall of surface- and groundwater, and temperature shifts over seasons or centuries. The Holocene is not a steady state, nor were the Ice Ages that came before it. The diversity that is clearly visible at Cedarburg reflects many variables at work and their influence over time. Ecological succession describes the process of change in the composition of species that exist in a certain area, the changing mix of plants and animals—some of which thrive, some which just manage to survive. Conditions may change gradually or abruptly and have short- or long-term effects. Each new species that finds a foothold in the community modifies its environment, creates its own ripple effect. As I followed the boardwalk through Cedarburg Bog, I could imagine the bog's evolution over millennia as the Ice Age loosened its grip and the warming earth invited a renewal of plant diversity.

We reached the farthest point on the trail, where the boardwalk forms a loop nestled into sedge meadow and bog. A bridge at the center of the loop affords enough elevation to gain a glimpse of the pattern of the string bog: Linear swaths of open wet ground filled with sedges alternate with narrow bands of stunted cedar and tamarack. The repeating parallel bands of wet and woody vegetation give the string bog its name and indicate the waterlogged nature of this unique peatland. While the water level across Cedarburg may fluctuate seasonally by as much as eighteen inches, the string bog stays perpetually saturated. Oxygen can penetrate only four to six inches below the surface. Temperatures in the peat are colder than in the uplands—another factor that limits plant growth—thus the diminutive size of the wizened trees that manage to survive. The waterlogged peat also inhibits decomposition, making available nutrients scarce. As a result, insectivorous plants flourish here, including pitcher plants, sundews, and bladderworts.

It was tempting to consider stepping off the elevated path and heading on foot deep into the heart of the bog. John described the students and researchers that conduct monitoring in the bog, all of them wearing hip waders and having the strength and stamina to trudge across soggy ground, and I was reminded of my earlier failure at navigating even a short stretch of bog-walking. So I sat on the edge of the boardwalk and tested the ground gently, easing myself onto the peat until I was standing on the softly undulating earth. It felt something like being in a small boat floating on the great swell of the sea. Below my feet was a layer of maybe eight or nine feet of peat. But its measure was not just in thickness of organic matter, it was a depth of time I stood upon. Here was the history of thousands of years—of seasonal cycles of frost and thaw, shedding and regrowth of leaves—and the passage of generations of trees, animals, and humans.

ANCHORAGE
COOK INLET
KENAI LOWLANDS
KENAI MOUNTAINS
CARIBOU HILLS
HOMER
GULF of ALASKA
MOOSE

ELEVEN

Climate Future

Kenai Lowlands, Alaska

Understanding the story of peatlands requires thinking on a longer timescale than years or decades. Looking back over ten thousand years of the Holocene, we see peatlands emerging and spreading across the postglacial world. This expansion was modest by some measures: Peatlands today cover only around 3 percent of the world's land surface. But their role in the global climate system—past and future—is outsized and underappreciated. Among the many diverse ecosystems on Earth, peatlands punch above their weight. The recognition of their importance, however, is beginning to grow. And in turn, we look anxiously to the future and wonder about the fate of peatlands in our modern era, what has been called the Anthropocene, a time in Earth's history when human activity is shaping the global environment in profound ways. Because this era feels new and different, looking to the past does not assure us of what lies ahead.

Rising temperatures and melting permafrost. Rainfall patterns becoming more extreme: wet places getting wetter, dry places getting drier. And everywhere, longer growing seasons and rising levels of carbon dioxide in the atmosphere. Since the end of the Pleistocene, temperature has been the primary influence in the development of peatlands in the northern latitudes. Rising temperatures since the retreat of the last ice sheets unleashed glacial meltwater and saturated vast expanses of freshly exposed soil. This created ideal conditions for the establishment of peatland pioneer species—*Sphagnum* mosses and sedges—and stimulated a green revolution across the previously barren landscape. Some scientists suggest that, under current climate trends, warmer temperatures and rising concentrations of atmospheric carbon dioxide could stimulate increased plant productivity, leading to greater peat accumulation and carbon storage, at least in higher latitude peatlands. The key is moisture; as long as sufficient water is available, keeping wetlands soggy and low in oxygen, peat can continue to accumulate. But when peatlands lose surface moisture (too much warmth, too little rainfall), microbial activity kicks into gear and decomposition begins to break down organic matter, releasing stored carbon.

Temperature and moisture are not the only variables that affect peatlands. A survey of peatland scientists published in 2021 explored the question of what factors have influenced peatland carbon stocks over the past ten thousand years, and how those drivers could tip the carbon balance of peatlands from sinks to sources over the next century. The survey queried forty-four peat experts about the "agents of change" that influence the fate of carbon stored in the world's peatlands, including sea level rise, fire, and land use change. Of particular concern are the forces at work that cause rapid carbon losses: permafrost thaw and peatland fires.

The dynamics of frozen soils are complex, and not all permafrost landscapes hold stores of peat. But permafrost conditions are an important influence in keeping carbon locked in soils by preventing decomposition. In the far north, across the high latitudes of North America and Eurasia, there are an estimated

1.7 million square kilometers of northern peatland bound in ice. With further increase in global temperatures, these permafrost lands could release their long-stored carbon and become a potent source of greenhouse gases. In one study, scientists predict that half of these frozen peatlands will be lost if the climate warms two degrees Celsius from preindustrial levels; at a higher rate of warming—six degrees Celsius—permafrost peatland would likely disappear altogether. The thawing is already underway, and its effects are dramatic.

As the climate warms, the upper layers of peat and soil become more active to decomposition, releasing carbon gases and potentially shifting the peatland from being a carbon sink to a carbon source. With further warming, permafrost melting below the soil surface can cause an abrupt collapse; a kind of sinkhole forms where solid ice gives way to liquid water. What was once frozen ground becomes a new terrain called *thermokarst,* a vast wetland dotted with lakes and ponds. The thawing of carbon-rich peat held in the permafrost presents the risk of what has been called a "carbon bomb," the rapid release of powerful greenhouses gases. Carbon is not only lost to the atmosphere through gas fluxes in the form of carbon dioxide and methane gases; it is also lost as dissolved carbon in water, flushing out of the peat into streams and lakes formed from the newly melted ice.

A warming climate drives another growing threat to peatlands. Milder winters, more frequent droughts, and the continuing impact of conversion and drainage of peatlands—all these trends contribute to lowering water tables and drying out the vast boreal region covering much of Canada and Alaska, making peatlands increasingly vulnerable to wildfire. Although fire is a natural part of boreal and tundra ecosystems, the effects of climate change and human activity are producing more frequent and severe wildfires. The record-breaking 2023 fire season in Canada burned an estimated 184,000 square kilometers (more than 70,000 square miles) and dimmed the sky with smoke for hundreds of miles. Many of these fires raged through boreal landscapes underlain by peatlands.

Densely packed with organic carbon, peat is a robust fuel source. It can ignite even in cold, wet conditions and can burn for weeks or months, producing dense smoke and emitting huge amounts of carbon. Peat often burns in smoldering fires, emitting carbon monoxide and methane as well as carbon dioxide. Intense, long-lasting fires can burn deeply into peatlands. As fire burrows below the surface, hot spots of smoldering peat (sometimes called "zombie fires") can persist through winter, insulated under blankets of snow, only to flare up again at the surface when the weather warms.

The changing nature of fires in the northern latitudes creates a series of feedback loops. For one, peatland fires create heat that adds to further drying of vegetation and soil; the more heat and drying, the more combustible the peat. Prolonged heat from fires can also accelerate permafrost melting and the spread of thermokarst landscapes. Peat fires change the surface topography of hummocks and hollows to something more like a moonscape of craters, a reshaping of the landscape that affects how, or whether, the peatland recovers. After a fire, mosses and wetland plants may not regenerate if the hydrology of the peatland has been drastically altered. Drier soils and lower water tables invite the encroachment of upland species such as aspen and birch. Deciduous trees take up more water than coniferous forest, adding to the feedback loop toward dry soils and increasing vulnerability to wildfire. The most worrisome feedback loop is the carbon lost to the atmosphere. When peat burns, a thousand years' worth of carbon can be released in the blaze of a single fire. That carbon adds to the concentration of greenhouse gases that are fueling climate change and the warming of the planet.

The collective view of peatland scientists in the 2021 survey was a prediction that peatlands will shift from carbon sinks to carbon sources by the end of this century. But they point out there are great uncertainties, because peatlands are not well represented in earth system models used for understanding the dynamics of climate change, and because peatlands sometimes show surprising resilience. Scientific literature on peatlands provides examples of losses and gains. In some cases, permafrost thaw is followed by rapid carbon losses and a slow recovery of the peatland ecosystem. In other studies, thawing permafrost creates warm, moist conditions that boost plant production, producing a net gain in carbon. How peatlands respond to fire is another line of research interest. One study examined fire history as part of peatland ecology in western Canada and found consistent evidence of a rapid and robust regrowth of *Sphagnum* mosses following low-intensity fires.

Are these glimmers of hope, or notions of wishful thinking? The past gives us perspective, but it is not a road map of what lies ahead. Wallace Stegner, in his novel *Angle of Repose,* wrote about looking through the lens of history with something like the Doppler effect: "The sound of anything coming at you—a train, say, or the future—has a higher pitch than the sound of the same thing going away."

Alaska in midsummer, and the sun shone night and day. One morning we woke to see wet ground; it had apparently rained in early morning, but hardly enough to dampen our pant legs when we walked through the grass. Many days, the enormous sky was laced with high clouds or trimmed with a ruffle of white over a distant range of mountains. The sun was always there, filling the landscape with energy that would sustain the plants and wildlife all through the long winter—a winter that will hopefully bring enough snow to replenish the rivers and underground streams next year. The cycle of seasons in Alaska is a highly magnified version of temperate climates. Extremes of daylight and darkness define summer and winter; powerful systems of ocean and air currents drive weather as they collide with the vertical rise of mountains. Water pulses through the landscape like a powerful vascular system, powering the rivers that fill with salmon that feed the great Alaskan brown bears. The water fills the soil too—vast stretches of boreal forest and taiga, endless horizons of shrubby fens and gaunt black spruce trees. The wetlands nurture an abundance of berry-producing shrubs (crowberries, blueberries, cloudberries) that burst with fruit in late summer and fill the bellies of those brown bears already fattened with fish. The feeding frenzy of summer is a necessity for birds, bears, moose, and all the animals that must store enough fat to endure the lean months of winter or provide enough energy to migrate elsewhere. The water that flows through the seasons is essential to the wetlands and forests, the berries and the birds, and keeps the cycles turning.

My travels in Alaska did not go as planned: My husband and I both fell sick with Covid in the first week of our trip. But we had a rental car and enough energy for walking, so we made the best of it, staying isolated from other people, convalescing in the freshness of open skies. Traveling counterclockwise around the Kenai Peninsula, we met its two faces. On the east side, the Kenai Mountains rise to six thousand feet, with dramatic expanses of glaciers and ice fields. At the head of the Kenai Fjords the sky was overcast, bathed in moisture from the Pacific. This eastern half facing Prince William Sound catches the marine air that rises, cools, and falls as rain or snow. In the western half of the peninsula, the Kenai Lowlands lie in a rain shadow, receiving less than half the precipitation of the mountains. Still, this is no desert: The Kenai Lowlands are dotted with lakes and rivers, and water spills from the interior through a rolling terrain of glacial moraines and kettle ponds. The landscape is clothed in boreal forests of spruce and trimmed with sedge fens, sustained by groundwater and glacial runoff. Below the surface, the organic matter that has accumulated here since the retreat of the last glacial age is stored as peat. Most of the peatlands in the Kenai Lowlands are fens, rather than true bogs, since they benefit from the abundance of water throughout the peninsula.

The long sunny days that illuminated the Kenai Lowlands are a reminder of the changes underway in the far north, where rising temperatures driven by climate change are increasing at a faster rate than in the midlatitudes. The growing season, marked by the span of frost-free nights, is getting longer. This might be thought of as a blessing for those animals trying to feed, reproduce, and prepare for winter. But the warmth is accompanied by changes in the hydrological system as the climate shifts to drier conditions. Scientists gauge this change in terms of the annual water balance, a measure of "effective moisture" described as precipitation minus evapotranspiration. Research in western Kenai shows a 60 percent decrease in the mean annual water balance over the past fifty years, since a major drought in 1968–69. The drying trend is triggering a visible change in the peat fens of the Kenai Lowlands: Trees are marching in, with the woody shrubs leading the way. Dwarf birch and black spruce trees are encroaching into sedge fens across the western peninsula as drier soils allow woody vegetation to become established in places that were previously too wet for them to put down roots.

My introduction to Kenai peat fens was illuminated by Ed Berg, a retired ecologist with many years of experience working in the Kenai National Wildlife Refuge and across the western peninsula. Ed is generous with his time and expertise, sharing his own research and references to studies in the Kenai—particularly those that focus on climate trends and the effects on peatlands.

"The spruce invasion of the wetlands began at the end of the Little Ice Age in the 1850s but has greatly accelerated since the 1970s with the general drying of the wetlands," explained Ed in one of his emails. This is not a gradual transition or part of a recurring pattern. "As one who has been looking at this landscape for forty-plus years," he wrote, "I tend to see it as changing rapidly, with human expansion, beetle-killed forests, melting icefields, and drying wetlands."

The effects of climate change are rapid, relative to the age of the peatlands. These fens began to accumulate peat as the ice sheets withdrew, more than ten thousand years ago. Clues to past climates are seen in peat cores that reflect environmental conditions as far back as the most recent extent of ice sheets, known as the Last Glacial Maximum. Peat coring involves pushing a three-inch metal tube down through the surface to withdraw a sample of the underlying peat. These earthen cylinders reveal a history of what plants grew and died in the fen over thousands of years. Because organic matter in the peat is only partly decayed, leaves, cones, and pollen can be identified, sometimes to a species level. The layers of peat, accumulating undisturbed, provide a chronology of the ecosystem, from the most recent at the top to the oldest layers at the depth of the peat. The absence of dead wood in the core samples from the Kenai Lowlands is notable; this indicates that over the past fourteen thousand years, the Kenai fens did not support forests but have been consistently dominated by herbaceous wetland plants. The oldest peat cores date back as far as eighteen thousand years before present. At least one significant warming period occurred during this time, with warmer summers five to six thousand years ago, but even this uptick in temperatures did not trigger an encroachment of woody plants into the wet fens.

Some scientists suggest that a warming climate and longer growing season may lead to greater productivity in woody species and thus increased carbon storage because trees and shrubs, with their layered structure of branches and leaves, have more surface area for photosynthesis. On the other hand, warming temperatures can activate decomposition in wetland soils, releasing carbon once safely stored in peat. The question is whether the carbon balance is a net gain (from enhanced growth of woody plants and the power of photosynthesis) or a net loss (from higher rates of plant respiration and biological decay). One study in the Kenai Lowlands measured carbon dioxide exchange in summer and winter in four different vegetation communities. The study sites fell along a moisture gradient, comparing moss and sedge wetlands to woody shrub and forest habitats. The result, after two years of monitoring, showed the woody plant communities were net sources of carbon dioxide, while the herbaceous wetlands were either neutral or net sinks.

The encroachment of woody species in the Kenai Lowlands triggers other ecological changes, some that may amplify the effects of climate change. Trees and shrubs are generally darker in color than sedges and mosses and absorb more heat, an effect called decreased albedo. The taller structure of woody plants also traps snow in winter. As snow accumulates around tree trunks and shrubs, it forms a layer of insulation that keeps soils warmer underneath, allowing more carbon loss during winter through respiration. Perhaps the greatest concern to the residents of the Kenai Lowlands is the increasing fire risk. The expanding forest of birch and spruce adds more fuel to the landscape, compounded by the drying of wetlands that once served as fire breaks. With warming temperatures, the official start of fire season has already moved up from the first of May to the first of April.

The peat fens of the Kenai Lowlands hold a vast store of carbon, growing in deepening layers for as much as fourteen thousand years. Aerial surveys indicate more than a quarter million acres of unforested wetlands covering peat deposits of varying thickness. How much carbon is sequestered here? And how does the transformation of ecological communities—from sedge fens to boreal forest—change the carbon flux in these landscapes? Professional biologists and citizen scientists in the Kenai Peninsula have been pursuing those questions through collaborative research and field studies.

Some of these local efforts have gained momentum through Homer Drawdown, a community initiative to promote locally based climate solutions. The project was inspired by the 2017 book by Paul Hawken, *Drawdown: The Most Comprehensive Plan Ever Proposed to Reverse Global Warming*. The book serves as a guide and reference for a global mission to advance efforts to reduce greenhouse gas emissions and aim for a profound turning point: "to achieve drawdown, the point when greenhouse gas levels in the atmosphere start to decline." When a group of Homer, Alaska, residents met in early 2020, they considered a broad range of climate actions they could undertake as a community; some of these focused on reducing greenhouse emissions, others looked at ways to enhance carbon sinks. The choice was an embrace of their own local peatlands in the Kenai Lowlands. Their goal is to "put peat on the map," both literally and figuratively, by documenting peat as an asset that should be considered as part of the landscape's resource value.

Homer Drawdown has generated a wealth of creative ideas that deepen the community's understanding and sense of stewardship of the southern Kenai peatlands. Volunteers are trained to collect data on the depths of local peat fens, providing information to better estimate the amount of stored carbon. Photo-monitoring helps to document visible changes in the wetland ecosystems. The project has an artistic as well as a scientific vision, with an artist-in-residence program and an "Art for Peat" exhibit at the local Pratt Museum. A peat-themed mural was installed in the Homer Airport Terminal in 2023, designed by Homer artist Kim McNett to be both "scientifically accurate and creatively imagined." The placement of this artwork might seem odd but for the fact that the airport sits, incongruously, adjacent to a large wetland complex, the Beluga Wetlands.

At the southern cusp of the Kenai Peninsula, blue-sky days gleamed with the sparkling waters of Kachemak Bay. On the eastern edge of the town of Homer, I walked the Calvin and Coyle Trail that meanders through spruce woods to a wide, open meadow. The morning was still and quiet but for the periodic drone of small planes taking off and landing at the nearby airstrip. The Beluga Wetlands receive the waters that drain from steep hillsides to the north into Beluga Lake and then into Beluga Slough, where fresh- and saltwater mix, emptying into the bay at Bishop's Beach. In spring and summer, the wetlands serve as resting and feeding areas for migratory waterfowl and shorebirds, including trumpeter swans and Aleutian terns. Close to three hundred acres of land have been designated as a critical habitat area, creating a buffer between the airport and the upland slopes, dotted with houses along East End Road and Skyline Drive.

As I wound through the forest, I listened for moose moving through the dark trees. I'd been cautioned to avoid surprising a moose mother and calf that might be foraging in the lush summer greenery. Public walking paths around Homer are well-signed with advice for keeping a safe and respectful distance from these long-limbed animals that can chase an unwary hiker up a tree, or worse, use their big feet as battering weapons. Where the trail neared the wetlands, I looked for moose prints in the moist earth but found none. The moose that I was looking out for are not just summer visitors. The Beluga Wetlands and adjacent uplands are important wintering grounds for a local moose population of about a hundred animals. Thickets of shrubby willows are a favorite and essential food source; the dense forest edge provides shelter from winter winds.

From the farthest reach of the loop trail I looked out over a sea of grasses bronzed by the sun and tried to visualize a winter landscape. Had I been there in December instead of June, I might have seen a moose high-stepping through snow or plowing through deep drifts. All movement takes energy, and calories are scarce in winter. A moose must work harder to browse, and her feeding range gets smaller. Because tree bark and woody branches are harder to digest than summer's soft leaves, she spends more time processing her rough diet. Unlike animals that migrate or hibernate, moose stay active all winter, and much of their days are spent ruminating food through the four stomachs in their digestive systems. A moose requires some ten thousand calories each day to endure the cold.

As I stood, half in sun and half in shade, a slight shiver ran through me—perhaps a lingering effect of my waning Covid symptoms or the imaginary chill of a winter day months in the future. Or perhaps I shuddered at the knowledge that temperatures in Alaska are warming twice as fast as in the lower forty-eight states and winters are warming more than summers. Observed and projected changes indicate evaporation rates increasing, snowmelt occurring earlier, more precipitation falling as rain than snow. The slower-paced planetary warming that began at the end of the Pleistocene released water that had been bound up in ice, water that flooded the scoured land and created the conditions for the early beginnings of peat to form. Millennia passed, and now an accelerated warming threatens to undo the work of the sedges and mosses that have been steadily absorbing carbon from the atmosphere and burying it away in the peat. The carbon cycle continues—as it has through the earth's long history—but at a hurried pace and with uncertain direction. A boreal chickadee perched above, quietly reminding me that I was in a world defined by its northern latitude and glacial history. The vast Kenai Lowlands seemed to have just emerged from the Ice Age, a landscape that appeared both old and new. But timeless it is not.

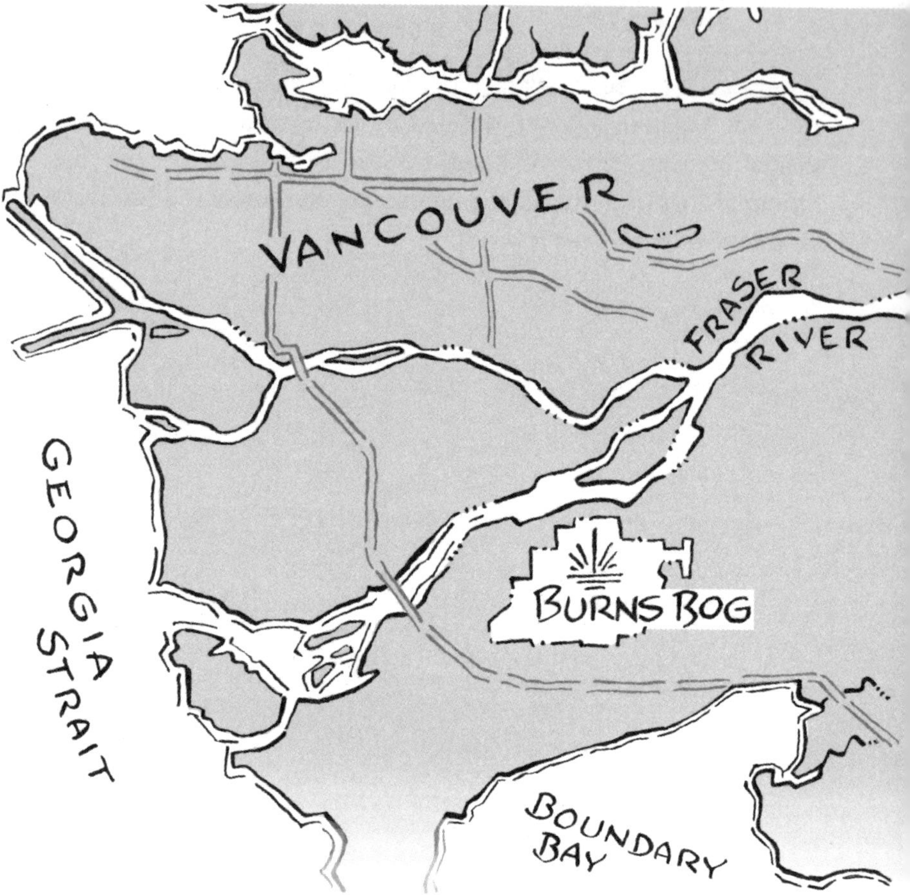
VANCOUVER
FRASER RIVER
GEORGIA STRAIT
BURNS BOG
BOUNDARY BAY

TWELVE

Resilience

Burns Bog, British Columbia

A bit of dried *Sphagnum* moss doesn't look like a living thing. A spidery bird claw, pale and brittle. But leave it in a small dish of water and wait a while. The curled feathers of its tiny arms unfurl, spreading into green fronds—not true leaves, but elegant pockets of plant tissue designed to absorb water. In its saturated state, *Sphagnum* can hold twenty times its dry weight in water. The water held within the moss is not just in idle storage; it combines with carbon dioxide from the air and stimulates the transformation of sunlight into food, carbohydrates that generate plant growth. Manna from heaven.

The nature of moss—its ability to spring back to life—is also its saving grace. Or it can be, if the water that was once withheld is replenished and reconnected. Water not only performs the resurrection miracle for the plant life that thrives in wet peat soils, it also restores the chemical processes that absorb and store carbon. *Sphagnum* mosses are emblematic of the adaptive power of peatland plants to tolerate environmental extremes and to modify their habitat to suit their needs. Other species, too, contribute to peatlands' capacity to adjust to changing conditions. For instance, microscopic communities of bacteria, fungi, and other organisms live in close-knit relationships with *Sphagnum* and can influence how mosses respond to fluctuations in water and temperature. A peatland community is inhabited by survivalists.

Resilience is the ability to withstand change, to endure through resistance or adaptation. Peatlands have persevered for millennia, in varying climates and geographies. The biodiversity of peatland communities, the detailed mosaics of their topography, the ways they preserve and transform organic matter into peat—all these qualities and characteristics underlie the resilient nature of peatlands. In ecological terms, peatlands demonstrate self-regulation: They adjust to the world and its changes, both internally and externally. What makes it difficult to predict how peatlands will respond to changing environmental conditions is the complex interplay of positive and negative feedbacks. Positive feedbacks reinforce or amplify change. Consider the encroachment of shrubs and trees into a nonforested peatland: Woody species take up more water from the soil, thereby lowering the water table, allowing the establishment of deeper root systems and inviting the establishment of more trees and shrubs. A negative feedback, in contrast, has a stabilizing effect. In peatlands, negative feedbacks enhance resilience by helping to maintain the functions of peat formation and carbon storage. One example is the physical changes in peat in response to drought. Under dry conditions, the water table declines and the structure of peat changes; the surface peat begins to decompose more quickly, but deeper down, the tiny spaces in the peat that hold water shrink or collapse. As a result, the peat becomes less permeable, and this decline in permeability slows the rate of water loss from the peatland, thus helping to moderate the effects of dry conditions.

Peatlands appear able to hold their own for long periods of time, decades to centuries, with negative feedbacks keeping the ecosystem in balance. These periods of stability can then be suddenly interrupted, triggered by some kind of positive feedback. The disruption may be subtle—say, a plant community shifting from a moss-dominated bog to a sedge-dominated fen, or vice versa. Or there may be a larger transformation of the ecosystem at work that alters the hydrology or the process of peat accumulation. Paleoecology (the study of past ecosystems and how they change over time) reveals that peatlands, when left undisturbed, are impressively resilient. But are the adaptations and feedbacks they have developed over millennia enough to withstand the slings and arrows of the twenty-first century? If peatlands are facing an existential moment, what can be done to protect them?

First, do no harm. The basic tenets of conservation are to avoid, minimize, and repair damage to a place or ecological community. In practice, there is long-running debate about how to prioritize among these actions. Is investment in restoring impaired ecosystems more urgent than saving those that are intact and undisturbed? Do the priorities change when the ecosystem represents an important element in the global carbon cycle? Scientists see both protection and restoration of peatlands as "natural climate solutions" (NCS for short), which are conservation measures that can make meaningful contributions to reducing and avoiding greenhouse gas emissions and increasing carbon removal from the atmosphere.

In a 2021 scientific paper, ecologists from The Nature Conservancy, Conservation International, and the World Wildlife Fund proposed an "NCS hierarchy" in which protection, management, and restoration were evaluated, considering the type of landscape (forest, grassland, wetland) and the potential results from conservation actions. These factors include how long it will take to achieve a climate benefit—that is, stopping the loss of carbon or resuming the uptake of carbon in an ecosystem. They also weigh the cost-effectiveness of different conservation strategies and the magnitude of the carbon sink. Also important to consider are things not as easily measured, such as biodiversity and cultural values. The conclusion of this analysis is that protection comes out on top. Avoiding damage to intact ecosystems lessens carbon emissions to the atmosphere and supports their ability to continue absorbing and storing carbon. This does not undermine the argument for restoration but instead adds a sense of urgency to do both: Repair damage, and safeguard what is unharmed.

Saving what we can means that size matters; larger areas of habitat are more resilient than small fragments. Biodiversity matters, too. Plant species adapted to peatlands have fine-tuned preferences and adaptations to temperature, acidity, and water chemistry. A diverse natural community includes those ecosystem engineers—like *Sphagnum*—that can shape the world around them. The tension between a resilient habitat and a vulnerable habitat is the core of the peatland story. Now, the conservation imperative is to recover from past damage while bracing for an uncertain future. Peatlands have an incredible capacity to endure, but only if we give them time and space to do so.

I stepped off the dusty farm road and followed my guide through a thicket of ferns and fragrant hedge of Labrador tea. We walked a path that Sarah Howie knows well. For sixteen years, Sarah followed this trail through Burns Bog every four weeks, checking monitoring wells placed throughout the Ecological Conservancy Area, a protected peatland of more than seven thousand acres. Sarah, a restoration ecologist with the City of Delta, and her colleague Markus Merkens with Metro Vancouver, made it possible for me to visit this rare gem of a peatland, which is generally off-limits to the public. The restricted access is both to protect the bog and the bog-walker. Years of past drainage and peat excavation have left ditches and depressions now overgrown with sedges and moss, a sort of peatland obstacle course. A misstep could quickly result in one or both feet trapped in a watery pit.

I spotted white PVC pipes poking up through the bog, rising above the low thicket like periscopes, as we pushed farther into the interior. Around a hundred monitoring wells have been installed since 2005 as part of a long-term effort to restore and protect Burns Bog. Assessing the progress of restoration requires tracking a crucial measure of the bog's health: depth to water table. The wells measure what is hidden below the surface, giving scientists a way of taking the pulse of the bog as it recovers. Data are collected year-round (mostly by scientists like Sarah, plodding through the *Sphagnum* moss on foot) and provide a record of the seasonal fluctuation of water depth during the rainy winter and spring and the dry summer months. The winter rains are abundant in southern British Columbia, with an average annual rainfall of forty-seven inches. July through September is known as the "moisture deficit season" when warmer temperatures increase evaporation and transpiration. These late summer months have the least rainfall, an average of less than five inches. As a result, more water is lost to the atmosphere than is received in precipitation.

Burns Bog is a true ombrotrophic bog: a peatland that receives water only from the atmosphere in rain, snow, or fog. If the water table is too low for too long—because of drainage or drought—the bog suffers. In an undisturbed bog, the water table is close to the surface, varying through cycles of wet and dry weather. When a bog has been ditched and drained for peat extraction, the water table is significantly lowered. The lower the depth to water table, the greater the changes to the bog's vegetation and chemistry. Monitoring the rise and fall of the water table throughout the annual cycle also reveals the elasticity of the peat itself. The water table fluctuates within the upper layer of peat, the top ten to twenty inches known as the *acrotelm*. (The deeper layers of peat, where anaerobic conditions prevail, are called the *catotelm*—based on the same Latin root for "catacomb.") As the bog absorbs winter rain, this layer becomes saturated and expands, raising the elevation of the bog surface. In summer, as the water table falls and evaporation increases, the peat contracts and lowers in height, mirroring the depth of the water table below. The flexibility of the peat and its capacity for water storage is essential for maintaining the peatland through the dry season. This slow process, known as "mire breathing," is an indicator of the peatland's resilience to the seasonal water cycle.

We stop to examine one of the monitoring wells. Sarah explains how seasonal changes in the elevation of the surface can be observed by how much of the PVC pipes are visible above the vegetation. As we stand under the hazy August sun, the bog surface is at its late summer ebb, and the white vinyl pipes stand out in the bog, easily seen from a distance. In wet winter months, the surface elevation may rise by a foot. Mire breathing (or to use the less poetic term, "bog surface oscillation") is an example of self-regulation in the ecosystem, a tool for the bog to adapt to environmental change.

We had begun our venture into Burns Bog from the western edge. Now, looking eastward across a hummocky expanse of low shrubs and underlying sedges and mosses, I could envision what was once part of a diverse network of peatlands that formed along the winding path of the Fraser River. A few historic peatlands remain of the Greater Lulu Island Bogs in what is now a nature park in the City of Richmond. Fragments of surviving bogs still lie along the upper river and its tributaries, including Langley Bog and the Pitt Polder. Burns Bog, too, has been diminished by the forces of change—roughly 40 percent of its original extent has been lost to agriculture and industrial development—but as a largely intact peatland, its size alone makes it a centerpiece of the ecological story of the Fraser River delta.

Some ten thousand years ago, as the Cordilleran ice sheet retreated from the west coast of North America, meltwater poured across the landscape toward the Pacific Ocean. The Fraser River flowed south into what is now known as Boundary Bay until about six thousand years ago, when the river shifted to the northwest, flowing into the Strait of Georgia. The broad delta of the Fraser River was fed by other rivers and received enormous volumes of sediment and silt, building a massive floodplain. In the dynamic environment of the river delta, plant communities adjusted to changing conditions; saltwater marsh turned to freshwater wetland, dense with sedges and grasses. The poorly drained delta land became the setting for peatlands to form as part of a vast wetland complex. By 3,500 years ago, peat was accumulating, underlain by a silt layer so that the peat mounded upward, forming a domed bog that holds its own store of acidic water above the regional water table. The changing conditions were ideal for true bog-associated plants to take hold, and *Sphagnum* mosses and Labrador tea soon became dominant.

The evolution of the bog did not occur on an empty stage. As the climate warmed, people migrated into the mouth of the Fraser River delta, making seasonal camps along the river and living on the bounty of land and sea. These were the ancestors of the Coast Salish, a diverse group of First Nation peoples linked by a shared language group. Settling here at least ten thousand years ago, they adapted to the changing environment and made modifications of their own, managing plant communities with fire. For thousands of years, the original inhabitants occupied the area in and around the Fraser River delta, leaving little to no trace of disturbance. The presence of Indigenous peoples is more than part of the history of the landscape. First

Nation communities continue to live in the region surrounding Burns Bog, including the Katzie First Nation, Kwantlen First Nation, Kwikwetlem First Nation, Musqueam Indian Band, Semiahmoo First Nation, Tsawwassen First Nation, and Tsleil-Waututh Nation.

The history of damage to Burns Bog and the neighboring peatlands began with European settlers moving into the Fraser River delta region in the early nineteenth century. Many of the immigrants came from farming communities; some had already struggled in midwestern and eastern parts of North America before moving farther west, seeking a promised land with abundant natural resources and a temperate climate. For homesteaders, turning the wild landscape into farmland meant removing trees and plowing prairies and peatlands. Forested swamplands were drained and transformed into croplands producing peas, cabbages, corn, and potatoes. In the drained peat, farmers found suitable conditions for growing cranberries and blueberries.

The same properties that make *Sphagnum* a miracle worker for building peatlands also make it appealing for agriculture. The value of peat is driving changes to bogs and fens across the landscape in two ways. The most wide-ranging effect is the drainage of peatlands to create farmland. In North America, an estimated twelve to fifteen thousand square miles of peatlands have been degraded by human activities, driven primarily by agriculture. A more localized but intensive impact is the removal of peat for use in horticulture as a growing medium in greenhouses and plant nurseries.

In the early twentieth century, settlers in the Fraser Delta began to harvest a different kind of crop: *Sphagnum* moss. Excavating wet peat by hand, spreading it out, and baling the dry, compact moss became profitable as "peat moss" products included insulation, packaging, and poultry litter. Peat extraction intensified in the 1940s; as weapons production ramped up during World War II, thousands of bales of peat were shipped to military sites in Nevada where the dried moss was used in the smelting process for manufacturing artillery shells. Toward the end of the war, demand for peat shifted to horticultural uses. Mining peat became more efficient with the use of hydraulic equipment replacing human labor. Two peat plants were constructed in Burns Bog, and a railway line was built to move the product to market. Eventually, the peat mining operations came to an end in the 1980s, but the evidence of some fifty years of intensive development remains as deep pools and drainage ditches. An estimated 40 percent of Burns Bog was affected by peat extraction. In many parts of the bog, the top three to six feet of surface peat were removed by peat mining. But the underlying peat remains, perhaps another ten to fifteen feet deep, ready to begin again in building new layers of *Sphagnum*. After a century of disturbance, Burns Bog has much healing to do.

In the forty years since peat mining ceased, some of the ditches have begun to recover on their own, with *Sphagnum* mosses filling the divots and scars left by excavation. But the process is slow, and progress depends on two necessary conditions. One is that undisturbed plant communities exist to recolonize the damaged areas of the bog. The other is to raise the "depth to water" by blocking the ditches. An ecosystem review of Burns Bog conducted in 2000 stated clearly: "Ditches that drain the core of the Bog must be blocked as soon as possible or the Bog will not survive." When restoration work began in 2007 the approach was simple: blocking ditches by starting in the center of the bog and working outward. To date, some 480 dams have been created by staff and contractors from the City of Delta. Almost all the work is done on foot and by hand; using vehicles would be impossible given the soggy terrain, and in any case would damage the peat they are working to protect.

Restoring the perimeter of the bog is especially tricky. The transition zone between the bog and adjacent upland known as a lagg is an important part of the wetland system that moderates the influences between the acidic, nutrient-poor peatland and the relative richness of the surrounding plant communities. In Burns Bog, much of the lagg has been lost to development, converted to farm fields, industrial parks, or freeway infrastructure. The drier edges of the Ecological Conservancy Area, where ditches have not been blocked, are shifting to pine forest with an understory of salal shrubs. Restoring this transition zone requires significant effort, when so little of the existing habitat remains undisturbed, but is further complicated by the need to prevent flooding and other impacts to neighboring properties.

The long-term effects of drainage in the bog pose additional challenges. As peat extraction and drainage lowered the water table, woody species such as lodgepole pines, birches, and salal encroached into the bog. Such trees are able to develop deeper roots belowground and grow tall and robust aboveground. As more trees became established, they drew up more water from the peat, worsening the drying effect and lowering the water table further. The transition of open bog to bog forest is difficult to reverse; some birch and pine trees may have to be removed by logging—a problem where vehicles cannot be used on the soft peat surface.

A fire in 2016 exacerbated the problem of trees encroaching in the bog. The heat of the fire triggered the release of massive amounts of seeds from the cones of lodgepole pines, giving rise to a small forest of woody saplings. To prevent the further spread of pines, in 2024 a local team from the Youth Climate Corps and CTS Youth Society went to work, cutting pines and removing the debris. The work party kickoff included traditional stories and local foods, contributed by community members from Tsawwassen and Kwantlen First Nations. The hands-on work of ecosystem restoration can be physically tiring, and yet uplifting. The restoration team, organized by the Metro Vancouver Regional Parks Foundation, removed more than thirty thousand young pine trees in just over five acres. For these Corps members, including youth from the Tsawwassen Nation, this is hands-on climate action—a contribution to the future.

Burns Bog is remarkable in its magnitude: The designated Ecological Conservancy Area encompasses more than eleven square miles of peatland lying within an urban landscape. Encircled by freeways, bordered by berry farms, industrial parks, and a landfill for the City of Vancouver, it has endured the passage of time and encroachment of the modern world. After decades of intensive drainage, ditches extended all the way into the heart of the bog. In the 1980s and 1990s, Burns Bog faced continuing threats from large-scale developments—a deep-sea port, industrial and residential projects, even a racetrack—but momentum was growing to save the bog. By 2000, public opposition to development proposals led to an independent scientific review that concluded that Burns Bog should be protected to maintain the ecological integrity of the peatland. A ballot referendum to determine public support for protecting Burns Bog passed by 75 percent of the vote. It took several more years to negotiate a purchase of the property and raise funds. Finally, in 2004, a coalition of municipal, provincial, and federal government agencies completed the initial purchase of five thousand acres of the peatland, setting it aside for conservation and committing to restore its wetland values to their former glory. In 2008, the Burns Bog Ecological Conservancy Area Management Plan was adopted. One of the notable aspects of the plan is the hundred-year time frame and its vision for Burns Bog as a "restored bog that is naturally evolving over time into a self-sustaining raised bog ecosystem."

The restoration of Burns Bog will take decades to recover the full functions of the ecosystem. This work demands patience, a greater challenge to sustain than the physical effort, financial commitment, and long-term monitoring that any sound wetland restoration effort involves. The first stage of ditch-blocking, undertaken as a kind of emergency triage to stem the bleeding, has yielded promising results. Sarah Howie notes that they have observed the water table rise near the sites where ditches were dammed and a stabilization of water levels across the area. Another encouraging sign is that interior ditches and peat harvest fields are beginning to see the regeneration of bog plant species.

After a half hour of steadily plodding through the bog, Sarah stopped to point out a crossroad, where the footpath intersected an old drainage ditch. A mound of earth formed a compact dam and served as a sort of footbridge across the ditch that was now flourishing with sedges and ferns. Nearby, we found the borrow pit—a section of peat that was dug out to create the dam. The small water-filled pocket was verdant green with *Sphagnum*; even in late summer it found a wet place to grow. The miracle of moss gives me hope.

Epilogue

Hope is a small thing, a human notion of what is possible. Its power is in how it can transform thought into action. Scientists, conservation advocates, policymakers—every actor on the stage has a part to play. The people supporting peatlands are as diverse as the peatlands themselves, and the actions they are taking are both pragmatic and creative. These actions can stem from different motivations, by various actors working alone or together: the local land trust that manages a ten-acre bog, the environmental activists that press for restrictions on peat mining, the alliance of governments committed to protecting peatlands across the world, the Indigenous people who have lived with peatlands for millennia.

There is conservation action: taking steps to protect peatlands from future harm. Some threats can be avoided—most important, preventing the physical disturbance of ditching and draining peatlands. Some past injuries can be mitigated, such as blocking drainage systems and restoring the natural hydrology that keeps peatlands wet. People and organizations engaged in conservation often struggle with competing priorities, preserving ecosystems that are intact and undisturbed while addressing the need to restore degraded peatlands and reverse the damage done.

There is scientific action: the continuing pursuit of a better understanding of how ecosystems work. Science can give us a clearer picture of how climate change affects peatlands and how peatlands, in turn, influence the climate both locally and globally. There is an infinite need for more data, generated from monitoring in the field and research in the lab. More data allows more sophisticated modeling, teasing out the myriad variables that influence whether peatlands will survive as carbon sinks or sources.

And there is policy action: creating rules, restrictions, and incentives that support the science, invest in conservation, and promote restoration. Government institutions do this at all levels—local, state, regional, national—and nongovernmental organizations influence how policies are made and implemented. Peatland protection can be woven into broader policies for sustainable land management, agriculture, and water resources. One of the challenges of policymaking is changing the course of direction, from a perspective that looked upon peatlands as wastelands to seeing the manifold benefits that wetlands provide.

Threaded throughout these actions is the virtue of stewardship: the enduring commitment to the survival of peatlands, inseparable from the fate of our own species. The deep connections between humans and the natural world is beautifully expressed in the concept of reciprocity. Robin Wall Kimmerer's book *Braiding Sweetgrass* inspired millions of readers with a profound but simple message: "We are bound in a covenant of reciprocity, a pact of mutual responsibility to sustain those who sustain us." Many peatland protection efforts are strengthened by blending science and traditional knowledge, engaging the Indigenous communities who hold a deep sense of place, a memory and knowledge of the water worlds encompassed in bogs and fens. Peatland conservation partners often work through networks, a joining of governmental and nongovernmental forces, academic researchers, and community leaders. These actions—conservation, science, policy, and stewardship—are building momentum as people work together at local, regional, and national scales.

In the high Andes of Peru, a collaboration of environmental groups and local communities is focused on habitat restoration in the Junín National Reserve that surrounds Lake Junín, also known as Lake Chinchaycocha. These high-elevation peatlands have suffered from overgrazing, peat extraction, fires, hydropower activities, and mining pollution. Led by regional conservation organizations and Wetlands International, the project is part of a larger initiative to protect and restore five peatland sites in Peru and Argentina, supported with funding from Green Choice, a Dutch energy company. At Lake Junín, the project team aims to scale up the restoration of degraded peatlands by blocking drainage ditches, reducing erosion with terracing, and protecting springs with fencing, improvements that help to sustain the ecosystem and the grazing-based livelihoods of the Aymara Indigenous community.

In Canada, the Mushkegowuk Council, representing seven First Nations communities of northern Ontario, is working with scientists from McMaster University, University of Toronto, and nongovernmental conservation partners on efforts to protect peatlands in the James Bay Lowlands—a vast area known to Indigenous citizens as "the Breathing Lands." Tribal community members learn methods for collecting peat samples for analysis of carbon content. These findings, combined with remote sensing and satellite data, will improve estimates of the immense carbon sink stored in the peatlands. Such information will also strengthen the case against proposed mining projects in the region that would threaten the lands and waters that sustain Indigenous communities.

In 2022, the government of Argentina formally declared the Peninsula Mitre in the southern tip of Tierra del Fuego as a national protected area. The 1.2 million hectare park preserves more than 80 percent of Argentina's known peatlands and represents the country's most significant carbon sink. The government's action prohibits mining and other resource extraction, military exercises and use of weapons, and introduction of exotic or invasive species. The announcement of the new law protecting Peninsula Mitre was applauded by many community and advocacy groups, including the Mane'kenk Association, representatives of local Indigenous communities who had been urging conservation action in this region for more than thirty years.

In the international sphere, a host of formal and informal coalitions are raising awareness of the importance of peatlands and the urgency to act for their protection. The value of peatlands as ecological landscapes was recognized in 1971 under the Ramsar Convention on Wetlands, one of the first landmark treaties created to support environmental goals. The Convention on Biological Diversity, adopted in 1992, further acknowledged the value of peatlands. In recent decades, advocates for wetland conservation have come to recognize the outsized role that peatlands play in the global carbon cycle. Preserving the ecosystem function of peatlands to absorb and store carbon is now understood to be a potent strategy for mitigating climate change, as evidenced by the efforts of some countries to incorporate peatlands into their national climate plans and commitments under international climate agreements.

A blend of conservation, science, and policymaking alliances highlight the importance of protecting and restoring peatlands in response to the growing need to address the linked climate and biodiversity crises. The Global Peatlands Initiative is one example of these diverse networks, formed in 2016 at the United Nations Framework Convention on Climate Change (UNFCCC) at its Conference of the Parties held in Marrakesh, Morocco. Its members reflect the conservation, science, and policy arenas of peatland protection: the United Nations Environment Programme and the Convention on Biological Diversity; more than ten universities representing Europe, Australia, Africa, and Canada; several private business and research partners; and at least a dozen nongovernmental conservation organizations, including the International Peatland Society, World Wildlife Fund, Wetlands International, The Nature Conservancy, Conservation International, and World Resources Institute.

And yet, even the growing international attention to peatlands is not enough to ensure their survival. An assessment published in 2025 describes a "mismatch" between the recognition of the value of peatlands and the scale of protected peatland landscapes. Researchers estimated that, worldwide, only 17 percent of peatlands are located in protected conservation areas. The status of protected peatlands compares poorly to other kinds of ecosystems: 42 percent of the global extent of mangrove habitats, 38 percent of tropical forests, and 50 percent of salt marshes lie within designated protected areas.

One important finding of the 2025 study is that more than one-fourth of global peatlands—some 1.1 million hectares, or about 425,000 square miles—are located in the lands and territories of Indigenous peoples. This overlapping geography, of peatlands and their inhabitants, highlights the power of stewardship. As one group of Canadian researchers noted in their study of Indigenous-led governance, "many of the areas prized by conservationists today have been stewarded by Indigenous Peoples for centuries to millennia." There is ample research and experience to show that conservation actions that engage local and Indigenous communities, incorporate place-based knowledge, and respect the value of reciprocity are those that are likely to endure over time.

Given what we know about the nature of peatlands and the threats they face, how do we use that knowledge? I have written the stories of peatlands as I see them, through the lens of three essential elements: water, carbon, time. Perhaps our response to this moment of uncertainty should be another trilogy: hope, action, stewardship. These gifts are already in our hands.

Acknowledgments

This book took six years of research, inquiry, and exploration—and still would not have been possible without the guidance and encouragement of many excellent scientists and conservation practitioners I consulted along the way. Many of these fine folks are named in the book; all deserve an additional shout-out of thanks.

In Minnesota, the centerpiece of my bog travels, I am grateful to Dr. Randall Kolka, US Forest Service Northern Research Station; Clinton Dexter-Nienhaus, Friends of Sax-Zim Bog; and Kristen Blann and Mark Felice, The Nature Conservancy. In British Columbia, my understanding of Burns Bog would not have been possible without help from Sarah Howie, City of Delta, and Markus Merkens, City of Vancouver. In Alaska, my mentor was Edward Berg, who generously shared his extensive experience in the ecology of the Kenai Peninsula. Insights from his own research on peatlands, both published and unpublished, were invaluable. In North Carolina, I am thankful to Sara Ward, US Fish and Wildlife Service; Eric Soderholm, The Nature Conservancy; and Curtis Richardson, Duke University, for their introduction to the ecology and history of pocosins. In

New Jersey, Emile DeVito and Russell Juelg steered me through the Pine Barrens to discover fascinating wetlands and hidden forests. In Wisconsin, my travels through the geologic past were guided by Sara Hotchkiss, University of Wisconsin, and John O'Donnell, Friends of Cedarburg Bog. In Maine, I was inspired by many peatlands under conservation protection, and especially by the research conducted by Daniel Grenier on The Nature Conservancy's Great Wass Island Preserve. In Pennsylvania, Roger Spotts, Kettle Creek Environmental Center, provided an excellent overview of Tannersville Cranberry Bog. In Peru, I was grateful to Monica Sofía Maldonado Fonkén, director of plant ecology at the Center for Ornithology and Biodiversity in Peru, for her introduction to high-elevation peatlands.

Writing a book requires more than an interesting subject. It demands time and attention through the slow process of writing, revising, and editing. For shepherding this project from manuscript to published book, I am sincerely indebted to Kristian Tvedten, Laura Westlund, Heather Skinner, Rachel Moeller, and Shelby Connelly at the University of Minnesota Press. Rob Hill and Denise Carlson added their professional care and attention to making this book shine. I am deeply grateful to Joy Drohan, editor extraordinaire and constant champion for getting the book out in the world. I owe many thanks, too, to Jeff Mathison for his amazing artwork.

Finally, this book is dedicated to my brothers Clay and Devan, and to my husband Kees.

Sources

1. FAR AND WIDE: BIG BOG, MINNESOTA

Crum, Howard. 1992. *A Focus on Peatlands and Peat Mosses.* University of Michigan Press.

Rotherham, Ian D. 2020. *Peatlands: Ecology, Conservation and Heritage.* Routledge.

Tiner, Ralph W. 1998. *In Search of Swampland: A Wetland Sourcebook and Field Guide.* Rutgers University Press.

United Nations Environment Programme (UNEP). 2022. "Global Peatlands Assessment—The State of the World's Peatlands: Evidence for Action Toward the Conservation, Restoration, and Sustainable Management of Peatlands." Main Report. Global Peatlands Initiative. Nairobi, Kenya.

Wright, H. E., Jr., Barbara A. Coffin, and Norman E. Aaseng, eds. 1992. *The Patterned Peatlands of Minnesota.* University of Minnesota Press.

2. LIVING ON THE EDGE: GREAT WASS ISLAND, MAINE

Barton, Andrew M. 2016. "Of Bogs and Pines: The Rare Nature of Great Wass Island." *Wild Seed* (January).

Barton, Andrew M., and Daniel J. Grenier. 2008. "Dynamics of Jack Pine at the Southern Range Boundary in Downeast Maine."

Canadian Journal of Forest Research 38 (4): 733–43. https://doi.org/10.1139/X07-176.

Barton, Andrew M., Alan S. White, and Charles V. Cogbill. 2012. *The Changing Nature of the Maine Woods.* University Press of New England.

Childs, Craig. 2018. *Atlas of a Lost World: Travels in Ice Age America.* Vintage Books.

Gawler, Susan, and Andrew Cutko. 2010. *Natural Landscapes of Maine: A Guide to Natural Communities and Ecosystems.* Maine Natural Areas Program, Maine Department of Conservation.

Lamb, Eric G., and William Megill. 2003. "The Shoreline Fringe Forest and Adjacent Peatlands of the Southern Central British Columbia Coast." *Canadian Field-Naturalist* 117 (2): 209–17.

McLaren, Duncan, Daryl Fedje, Angela Dyck, Quentin Mackie, Alisha Gauvreau, and Jenny Cohen. 2018. "Terminal Pleistocene Epoch Human Footprints from the Pacific Coast of Canada." *PLoS ONE* 13 (3): e0193522. https://doi.org/10.1371/journal.pone.0193522.

Rotbarth, Ronny, David J. Cooper, Logan Berner, and Roman Dial. 2023. "The World's Boreal Forests May Be Shrinking as Climate Change Pushes Them Northward." *The Conversation.* November 3, 2023. https://theconversation.com/the-worlds-boreal-forests-may-be-shrinking-as-climate-change-pushes-them-northward-211314.

Weidensaul, Scott. 2016. *Mountains of the Heart: A Natural History of the Appalachians.* Fulcrum Publishing. [excerpt from page 126, Twentieth Anniversary Edition]

3. HIGH AND LOW: MARCAPOMACOCHA, PERU

Draper, Frederick C., Katherine H. Roucoux, Ian T. Lawson, et al. 2014. "The Distribution and Amount of Carbon in the Largest Peatland Complex in Amazonia." *Environmental Research Letters* 9 (12): 1–12. https://doi.org/10.1088/1748-9326/9/12/124017.

Fraser, Barbara. 2012. "Melting in the Andes: Goodbye Glaciers." *Nature* 491 (7423) (November 8): 180–82. https://doi.org/10.1038/491180a.

Lähteenoja, Outi, and Susan Page. 2011. "High Diversity of Tropical Peatland Ecosystem Types in the Pastaza-Marañón Basin, Peruvian Amazonia." *Journal of Geophysical Research* 116 (G2). https://doi.org/10.1029/2010JG001508.

Maldonado Fonkén, M. S. 2014. "An Introduction to the Bofedales of the Peruvian High Andes." *Mires and Peat* 15 (05): 1–13. https://doi.org/10.19189/001c.128519.

Mark, Bryan G., Adam French, Michel Baraer, et al. 2017. "Glacier Loss and Hydro-Social Risks in the Peruvian Andes." *Global and Planetary Change* 159 (December): 61–76. https://doi.org/10.1016/j.gloplacha.2017.10.003.

Rydin, Håkan, and John K. Jeglum. 2013. *The Biology of Peatlands.* Oxford University Press.

Salvador, Flor, Jorge Monerris, and Line Rochefort. 2015. "Peatlands of the Peruvian Puna Ecoregion: Types, Characteristics and Disturbance." *Mires and Peat* 15 (03): 1–17. https://doi.org/10.19189/001c.128517.

United Nations Environment Programme (UNEP). 2022. "Global Peatlands Assessment—The State of the World's Peatlands: Evidence for Action Toward the Conservation, Restoration, and Sustainable Management of Peatlands." Main Report. Global Peatlands Initiative. Nairobi, Kenya.

Verzijl, Andres, and Silvano Guerrero Quispe. 2013. "The System Nobody Sees: Irrigated Wetland Management and Alpaca Herding in the Peruvian Andes." *Mountain Research and Development* 33 (3): 280–93. https://doi.org/10.1659/MRD-JOURNAL-D-12-00123.1.

4. WATER WORLDS: TANNERSVILLE CRANBERRY BOG, PENNSYLVANIA

Cox, Donald D. 2002. *A Naturalist's Guide to Wetland Plants: An Ecology for Eastern North America.* Syracuse University Press.

Davis, Ronald B. 2016. *Bogs and Fens: A Guide to the Peatland Plants of the Northeastern United States and Adjacent Canada.* University Press of New England.

Eastman, John. 1995. *The Book of Swamp and Bog: Trees, Shrubs, and Wildflowers of Eastern Freshwater Wetlands.* Stackpole Books.

Schnell, Donald E. 2002. *Carnivorous Plants of the United States and Canada.* Timber Press.

5. BOG BUILDERS: ORONO BOG, MAINE

Dickinson, Emily. 1896. *Poems: Third Series.* Edited by Mabel Loomis Todd. Roberts Brothers.

Johnson, Charles W. 1985. *Bogs of the Northeast.* University Press of New England.

Kettridge, Nicholas, Xavier Comas, Andrew Baird, et al. 2008. "Ecohydrologically Important Subsurface Structures in Peatlands Revealed by Ground-Penetrating Radar and Complex Conductivity Surveys." *Journal of Geophysical Research* 113 (G4): 1–15. https://doi.org/10.1029/2008JG000787.

Kimmerer, Robin Wall. 2003. *Gathering Moss: A Natural and Cultural History of Mosses.* Oregon State University Press. [excerpt from page 21, first edition paperback]

Longcore, Jerry R., James E. Bird, and Robert Klose. 2019. *The Bog Walker's Companion: A Guide to the Orono Bog Boardwalk.* University of Maine Press.

6. OUTFLOW: PINE BARRENS, NEW JERSEY

Boyd, Howard P. 1991. *A Field Guide to the Pine Barrens of New Jersey.* Plexus Publishing.

Boyd, Howard P. 1997. *A Pine Barrens Odyssey: A Naturalist's Year in the Pine Barrens of New Jersey.* Plexus Publishing.

Foreman, Richard T. T., ed. 1998. *Pine Barrens: Ecosystem and Landscape.* Rutgers University Press.

Mylecraine, Kristin A., and George L. Zimmermann. 2000. *Atlantic White-Cedar: Ecology and Best Management Practices Manual.* New Jersey Department of Environmental Protection, Division of Parks and Forestry.

Playfair, Susan. 2014. *America's Founding Fruit: The Cranberry in a New Environment.* University Press of New England.

Wessels, Tom. 1997. *Reading the Forested Landscape: A Natural History of New England.* Countryman Press.

7. SINKS AND SOURCES: POCOSIN LAKES, NORTH CAROLINA

Hazen, Robert M. 2019. *Symphony in C: Carbon and the Evolution of (Almost) Everything.* W. W. Norton & Company.

Lee, David S. 1986. "Pocosin Breeding Bird Fauna." *American Birds* 40 (5): 1263–73.

Nahlik, A. M., and M. S. Fennessy. 2016. "Carbon Storage in US Wetlands." *Nature Communications.* December 13, 2016. https://doi.org/10.1038/ncomms13835.

Richardson, Curtis J. 2018. "Chapter 52: Pocosins (USA)." In *The Wetland Book: II. Distribution, Description and Conservation,* edited by C. Max Finlayson, G. Randy Milton, R. Crawford Prentice, and Nick C. Davidson. Springer. https://doi.org/10.1007/978-94-007-4001-3_144.

US Fish and Wildlife Service. 2020. "Draft Water Management Plan and Environmental Assessment for Pocosin Lakes National Wildlife Refuge." June 2020. https://www.fws.gov/refuge/wwd/water_mgt_plan.html.

8. COUNTING CARBON: MARCELL EXPERIMENTAL FOREST, MINNESOTA

Graham, J. D., D. M. Ricciuto, N. F. Glenn, and P. J. Hanson. 2022. "Incorporating Microtopography in a Land Surface Model and Quantifying the Effect on the Carbon Cycle." *Journal of Advances in Modeling Earth Systems* 14 (2): e2021MS002721. https://doi.org/10.1029/2021MS002721.

Griffiths, Natalie A., Paul J. Hanson, Daniel M. Ricciuto, et al. 2017. "Temporal and Spatial Variation in Peatland Carbon Cycling and Implications for Interpreting Responses of an Ecosystem-Scale

Warming Experiment." *Soil Science Society of America Journal* 81 (6): 1668–88. https://doi.org/10.2136/sssaj2016.12.0422.

Hanson, Paul J., Natalie A. Griffiths, Colleen M. Iversen, et al. 2020. "Rapid Net Carbon Loss from a Whole-Ecosystem Warmed Peatland." AGU *Advances* 1 (3): e2020AV000163. https://doi.org/10.1029/2020AV000163.

Kolka, R., C. Trettin, W. Tang, et al. 2018. "Chapter 13: Terrestrial Wetlands." In *Second State of the Carbon Cycle Report (SOCCR2): A Sustained Assessment Report,* edited by N. Cavallaro, G. Shrestha, R. Birdsey, et al. US Global Change Research Program. https://web.archive.org/web/20250630063631/https://carbon2018.globalchange.gov/chapter/13/.

Nabokov, Vladimir. 1973. *Strong Opinions.* Vintage Books. [excerpt from page 168, first Vintage International Edition]

US Global Change Research Program. 2018. *Second State of the Carbon Cycle Report (SOCCR2): A Sustained Assessment Report.* Edited by N. Cavallaro, G. Shrestha, R. Birdsey, et al. https://web.archive.org/web/20250630032823/https://carbon2018.globalchange.gov/.

9. RECOVERY: SAX-ZIM BOG, MINNESOTA

Bjornerud, Marcia. 2018. *Timefulness: How Thinking Like a Geologist Can Help Save the World.* Princeton University Press. [excerpt from page 157, first edition paperback]

Chimner, Rodney A., David J. Cooper, Frederic C. Wurster, and Line Rochefort. 2016. "An Overview of Peatland Restoration in North America: Where Are We After 25 Years?" *Restoration Ecology* 25 (2): 283–92. https://doi.org/10.1111/rec.12434.

González, Eduardo, and Line Rochefort. 2014. "Drivers of Success in 53 Cutover Bogs Restored by a Moss Layer Transfer Technique." *Ecological Engineering* 68 (July): 279–90. https://doi.org/10.1016/j.ecoleng.2014.03.051.

Gorham, Eville, and Line Rochefort. 2003. "Peatland Restoration: A Brief Assessment with Special Reference to *Sphagnum* Bogs." *Wetlands Ecology and Management* 11 (February): 109–19. https://doi.org/10.1023/A:1022065723511.

Günther, Anke, Alexandra Barthelmes, Vytas Huth, et al. 2020. "Prompt Rewetting of Drained Peatlands Reduces Climate Warming Despite Methane Emissions." *Nature Communications* 11 (1644). https://doi.org/10.1038/s41467-020-15499-z.

Hugron, Sandrine, Mélina Guêné-Nanchen, Noémie Roux, Marie-Claire LeBlanc, and Line Rochefort. 2020. "Plant Reintroduction in Restored Peatlands: 80% Successfully Transferred—Does the Remaining 20% Matter?" *Global Ecology and Conservation* 22 (June). https://doi.org/10.1016/j.gecco.2020.e01000.

Prince, Hugh. 1997. *Wetlands of the American Midwest: A Historical Geography of Changing Attitudes.* University of Chicago Press.

Waddington, James M., Janina Plach, Jason P. Cagampan, Maria Lucchese, and Maria Strack. 2009. "Reducing the Carbon Footprint of Canadian Peat Extraction and Restoration." *AMBIO: A Journal of the Human Environment* 38 (4): 194–200. https://doi.org/10.1579/0044-7447-38.4.194.

10. CLIMATE PAST: KETTLE MORAINE, WISCONSIN

Ireland, Alex W., Robert K. Booth, Sara C. Hotchkiss, and Jennifer E. Schmitz. 2012. "A Comparative Study of Within-Basin and Regional Peatland Development: Implications for Peatland Carbon Dynamics." *Quaternary Science Reviews* 61 (February): 85–95. https://doi.org/10.1016/j.quascirev.2012.10.035.

Ireland, Alex W., Robert K. Booth, Sara C. Hotchkiss, and Jennifer E. Schmitz. 2012. "Drought as a Trigger for Rapid State Shifts in Kettle Ecosystems: Implications for Ecosystem Responses to Climate Change." *Wetlands* 32 (July): 989–1000. https://doi.org/10.1007/s13157-012-0324-6.

Ireland, Alex W., and Robert K. Booth. 2011. "Hydroclimatic Variability Drives Episodic Expansion of a Floating Peat Mat in a North American Kettlehole Basin." *Ecology* 92 (1): 11–18. https://doi.org/10.1890/10-0770.1.

Reinartz, James A. 1985. "A Guide to the Natural History of the Cedarburg Bog: Part One." *Field Station Bulletin* 18 (2): 1–48.

Sherman, Eric, and Andrew Hanson III, eds. 2008. *Along Wisconsin's Ice Age Trail.* The University of Wisconsin Press.

Spoolman, Scott. 2018. *Wisconsin State Parks: Extraordinary Stories of Geology and Natural History.* Wisconsin Historical Society Press.

Thorson, Robert M. 2009. *Beyond Walden: The Hidden History of America's Kettle Lakes and Ponds.* Walker Publishing Company.

11. CLIMATE FUTURE: KENAI LOWLANDS, ALASKA

Berg, Edward E. Forthcoming. *A Landscape History of the Southwestern Kenai Peninsula.*

Berg, Edward E., Kacy McDonnell Hillman, Roman Dial, and Allana DeRuwe. 2009. "Recent Woody Invasion of Wetlands on the Kenai Peninsula Lowlands, South-Central Alaska: A Major Regime Shift After 18,000 Years of Wet *Sphagnum*-Sedge Peat Recruitment." *Canadian Journal of Forest Research* 39 (11): 2033–46. https://doi.org/10.1139/X09-121.

Homer Soil and Water Conservation District. 2013. "Beluga Planning Area, Homer—Volume 1." June 2013. https://www.homerswcd.org/user-files/pdfs/Beluga-Planning-Area-Homer-Vol1.pdf.

Homer Soil and Water Conservation District and Kenai Peninsula Wetlands Working Group. 2014. "Kenai Peninsula Wetlands: A Guide for Everyone." October 2014. http://www.homerswcd.org/user-files/pdfs/KPWetlandsGuideForEveryone.pdf.

Hugelius, Gustaf, Julie Loisel, Sarah Chadburn, et al. 2020. "Large Stocks of Peatland Carbon and Nitrogen Are Vulnerable to Permafrost Thaw." PNAS 117 (34). https://doi.org/10.1073/pnas.1916387117.

Ives, Susan L., Patrick F. Sullivan, Roman Dial, Edward E. Berg, and Jeffrey M. Welker. 2013. "CO_2 Exchange Along a Hydrologic Gradient in the Kenai Lowlands, AK: Feedback Implications of Wetland Drying and Vegetation Succession." *Ecohydrology* 6 (1): 38–50. https://doi.org/10.1002/eco.274.

Kachemak Bay National Estuarine Research Reserve. "Climate Science of Kachemak Bay and the Kenai Peninsula." http://trnerr.org/wp-content/uploads/2016/04/Climate-science_Kachemak-Bay_Kenai-Peninsula.pdf.

Klein, Eric, Edward E. Berg, and Roman Dial. 2005. "Wetland Drying and Succession Across the Kenai Peninsula Lowlands, South-Central Alaska." *Canadian Journal of Forest Research* 35 (8): 1931–41. https://doi.org/10.1139/x05-129.

Kuosmanen, Niina, Minna Väliranta, Sanna Piilo, Eeva-Stiina Tuittila, Pirita Oksanen, and Tuomo Wallenius. 2023. "Repeated Fires in Forested Peatlands in Sporadic Permafrost Zone in Western Canada." *Environmental Research Letters* 18 (9). https://doi.org/10.1088/1748-9326/acf05b.

Loisel, J., A. V. Gallego-Sala, M. J. Amesbury, et al. 2021. "Expert Assessment of Future Vulnerability of the Global Peatland Carbon Sink." *Nature Climate Change* 11 (December). https://doi.org/10.1038/s41558-020-00944-0.

Nelson, K., D. Thompson, C. Hopkinson, R. Petrone, and L. Chasmer. 2021. "Peatland-Fire Interactions: A Review of Wildland Fire Feedbacks and Interactions in Canadian Boreal Peatlands." *Science of the Total Environment* 769 (May). https://doi.org/10.1016/j.scitotenv.2021.145212.

Stegner, Wallace. 1970. *Angle of Repose.* The Modern Library. [excerpt from page 14, Modern Library Edition hardcover]

12. RESILIENCE: BURNS BOG, BRITISH COLUMBIA

Cook-Patton, Susan C., C. Ronnie Drever, Bronson W. Griscom, et al. 2021. "Protect, Manage and Then Restore Lands for Climate

Mitigation." *Nature Climate Change* 11: 1027–34. https://doi.org/10.1038/s41558-021-01198-0.

Giblett, Rod. 2014. *Canadian Wetlands: Place and People.* University of Chicago Press.

Hebda, Richard J., Kent Gustavson, Karen Golinski, and Alan M. Calder. 2000. "Burns Bog Ecosystem Review Synthesis Report for Burns Bog, Fraser River Delta, South-western British Columbia, Canada." Environmental Assessment Office. https://www2.gov.bc.ca/assets/gov/environment/natural-resource-stewardship/environmental-assessments/eao-project-reviews/burns-bog-syntheses-report.pdf. [excerpt from page vi]

Howie, Sarah A., and Richard J. Hebda. 2018. "Bog Surface Oscillation (Mire Breathing): A Useful Measure in Raised Bog Restoration." *Hydrological Processes* 32 (11): 1518–30. https://onlinelibrary.wiley.com/doi/abs/10.1002/hyp.11622.

Howie, S. A., H. J. van Meerveld, and R. J. Hebda. 2016. "Regional Patterns and Controlling Factors in Plant Species Composition and Diversity in Canadian Lowland Coastal Bogs and Laggs." *Mires and Peat* 18 (23). https://doi.org/10.19189/MaP.2016.OMB.242.

Howie, S. A., P. H. Whitfield, and R. D. Moore. 2020. "Plant Community Type Is an Indicator of the Seasonal Moisture Deficit in a Disturbed Raised Bog." *Ecohydrology* 13 (4). https://onlinelibrary.wiley.com/doi/abs/10.1002/eco.2209.

Loisel, Julie, and Angela Gallego-Sala. 2022. "Ecological Resilience of Restored Peatlands to Climate Change." *Communications Earth & Environment* 3 (208). https://doi.org/10.1038/s43247-022-00547-x.

Metro Vancouver. "Burns Bog Ecological Conservancy Area Management Plan." May 2007. https://metrovancouver.org/services/regional-parks/Documents/burns-bog-management-plan.pdf. [excerpt from page 7]

Nyberg, M., T. A. Black, R. Ketler, et al. 2022. "Impacts of Active Versus Passive Re-Wetting on the Carbon Balance of a Previously Drained Bog." *Journal of Geophysical Research: Biogeosciences* 127 (9).

https://agupubs.onlinelibrary.wiley.com/doi/full/10.1029/2022JG006881.

Page, S. E., and A. J. Baird. 2016. "Peatlands and Global Change: Response and Resilience." *Annual Review of Environment and Resources* 41: 35–57. https://doi.org/10.1146/annurev-environ-110615-085520.

Waddington, J. M., P. J. Morris, N. Kettridge, G. Granath, D. K. Thompson, and P. A. Moore. 2015. "Hydrological Feedbacks in Northern Peatlands." *Ecohydrology* 8 (1): 113–27. https://doi.org/10.1002/eco.1493.

EPILOGUE

Artelle, Kyle A., Melanie Zurba, Jonaki Bhattacharyya, et al. 2019. "Supporting Resurgent Indigenous-Led Governance: A Nascent Mechanism for Just and Effective Conservation." *Biological Conservation* 240 (December). https://doi.org/10.1016/j.biocon.2019.108284.

Austin, Kemen G., Paul R. Elsen, Euridice N. Honorio Coronado, et al. 2025. "Mismatch Between Global Importance of Peatlands and the Extent of Their Protection." *Conservation Letters* 18 (1): e13080. https://doi.org/10.1111/conl.13080.

Kimmerer, Robin Wall. 2013. *Braiding Sweetgrass: Indigenous Wisdom, Scientific Knowledge, and the Teachings of Plants.* Milkweed Editions. [excerpt from page 382, first edition paperback]

Index

JENNIFER DE MOOY has worked in conservation, environmental protection, and climate policy for more than forty years. For two decades she planned and implemented projects with The Nature Conservancy to protect and restore natural habitats across California, and she has been involved with statewide climate change adaptation and mitigation in Delaware.